CONTENTS

INTRODUCTION

BY SAXBY SMART,
BRILLIANT SCHOOLBOY DETECTIVE

IF YOU'VE READ ANY of my collections of case files, you'll know that as well as solving mysteries for the pupils and staff of St Egbert's School, I'm also a great fan of detective stories. In fact, thinking about it, most of the books I read involve detectives in one way or another. There's a small pile of them on my bedside cabinet right now. Books, I mean, not detectives.

A while ago, my great friend George 'Muddy' Whitehouse (our school's resident gizmo genius, and possibly the most oil-and-mud-stained kid in the whole world) was helping me sort some notes out in my garden shed. It's in the shed that I have my desk, my extensive files of case notes, and my Thinking Chair, the battered old leather armchair in which I sit and ponder, detective-style, on whatever mind-mangling mystery has recently come my way.

We were re-organising the contents of my filing cabinet. Muddy was about to file my notes on *The Case of the Mexican Diamond* under *Robberies*, when I said it ought to go under *Blackmail* because that was the whole reason it was nicked in the first place.

'Y'know, Saxby,' said Muddy, scratching at some dried-up egg on his school pullover, 'what you don't know about detectives could fill a book. No, wait a mo, that's not right . . . Er, what you know wouldn't not be enough to make a . . . No, that's not it, either . . . Umm, oh you know what I mean.'

I did. And it got me thinking. In the Sherlock Holmes stories (see page 171), Holmes is always going on about how he's going to write a textbook on detective work one day, but he never gets around to it. I thought to myself: No way am I going to make the same mistake!

So shortly after that, I got to work. And the book you're now holding is the result.

There's stuff about detectives in fiction, and there's stuff about detectives in real life. There's stuff about some of the most notorious events in criminal history, and there are lessons and practical guides covering aspects of How to Be A Detective Yourself (based on my extensive experience of crime-busting!).

Best wishes,

Saxby Smart

EXHIBIT A:
CASE STUDIES!

Notorious Crimes and Criminals of the Past

YOU COULD FILL ENTIRE libraries with reports and investigations into famous crimes! This selection is just the tip of a very large iceberg, so it isn't meant to be a Top Ten Crimes, or anything like that. It's a (roughly chronological) look at just a few crimes and criminals that have caught my eye: some of them were the first – or worst! – of their kind, some of them changed the way law and order operates and some were the inspiration for famous detective stories. Here are murderers, thieves, gangsters, forgers and thugs. Enjoy!

Saxby

ISAAC NEWTON AND THE COIN CLIPPERS

In the mid-seventeenth century, one William Chaloner was born in rural Warwickshire and from a very young age proved to be a wrong 'un. His parents found him uncontrollable and he was always getting mixed up in some criminal scheme or other.

He was sent to be an appentice in Birmingham, in the hope that having a trade might help him see the error of his ways. However, Birmingham was home to a large number of forgers and soon Chaloner did indeed have a trade: he was a skilled maker of fake coins.

Important Background Information

In the 1680s and 1690s, Britain was in big trouble. The country's currency was the target of crooks in two ways:

1. Coins made before 1662 could be 'clipped' (the edges could be snipped or shaved away and the shavings melted down, either to make fake coins or to be sold).

2. Coins made after 1662, which were better made and had decorated edges to show up any clipping, were simply copied.

'Coiners', as they were known, clipped and copied so much that the country's whole economy was in danger. Millions of British coins were fake.

At some point in the 1680s, William Chaloner moved to London and quickly got up to his old tricks. He had what one writer at the time called 'the best knack at tongue-pudding', meaning he was charming and persuasive, and for a while he tried to sell fake medicine and pretended he could see into the future. But his coining skills were second to none and it didn't take long for him to become the nation's busiest maker of forged currency.

Chaloner was so successful that he could soon afford a house in the country, a posh carriage to get around in and the best quality clothes. He was nearly thrown into prison on a number of occasions, but time and time again that 'tongue-pudding' of his allowed him to weasel out of trouble. He would testify against other criminals in return for a pardon, or spread false rumours to deflect suspicion, or simply lie his way out of a tight spot.

By 1696, with the country in the middle of a very expensive war with France, the coining problem was becoming a very serious issue for the government. Enter an unlikely hero to save the day: Isaac Newton.

Newton was the most important scientific and mathematical thinker of his day, and is often regarded as the founder of modern science. He was asked to become Warden of the Royal Mint (the organisation allowed to make – 'mint' – coins and banknotes in the UK), in the hopes he might solve the problem.

Newton might seem like a peculiar choice for such a job. He was a brilliant scholar, but not exactly a dynamic man of action. But in addition to a razor-sharp mind, he paid great attention to detail and never gave up once he was on the trail of something. So, in fact, Isaac Newton had the perfect qualities for a detective!

Apart from reorganising the Royal Mint itself, Newton put ending the coining career of William Chaloner at the top of his To Do list. By now, Chaloner had started to forge banknotes and lottery tickets, which were new inventions, and Newton was determined to catch him.

Newton's detective work was slow and methodical. Using informants and witnesses, Newton gradually built evidence against Chaloner, while taking care that Chaloner himself didn't get to hear about the investigation.

Chaloner was finally arrested in 1699 and charged with High Treason. Newton's thoroughness ensured that there was no way Chaloner could wriggle out of it this time.

Rather like Jonathan Wild a few years later (see page 21), Chaloner tried every trick in the book to avoid his fate. While in Newgate prison, Chaloner pretended to go mad and even wrote letters begging to be let off. But William Chaloner was hanged at Tyburn in March 1699.

One of the grovelling letters William Chaloner wrote to Isaac Newton from Newgate prison (complete with dodgy seventeenth century spellings and rubbish punctuation!):

> *O Dear Sr do this mercifull deed O my offending you has brought this upon me O for Gods sake if not mine Keep me from being murdered O dear Sr nobody can save me but you O God my God I shall be murdered unless you save me O I hope God will move your heart with mercy pitty to do this thing for me.*
>
> *I am Your near murdered humble Servant.*

Newton didn't reply.

SMUGGLERS

Governments made people pay money – tax – on goods that they brought into (or out of) the country. Smugglers tried to avoid paying this tax by sneaking the goods in (or out).

Some of the earliest taxes charged in Britain were on wool. King Edward I began taxing all wool leaving the country in 1275. No sooner was the tax imposed than smugglers known as 'owlers' began finding ways of avoiding it!

But smuggling wasn't a big problem until the 1700s when Britain was fighting one war after another – usually with France. The government needed to pay for the wars and so it placed taxes on more and more items that were traded abroad: silk, lace, spices, wine, tea, perfume . . . By 1760, there were 800 items you had to pay 'excise duty' on. By 1810, there were well over 2000.

Smuggling, or 'free-trading' as it was often called at the time, spread like wildfire all around the British coast. Sometimes entire communities would be involved in smuggling in one way or another, as the dreadful poverty of most people made the potential rewards of law-breaking look very attractive. Even those who were well-off got involved. It was often rich folk who financed smuggling trips, paying for the illegal cargo in the first place.

Often, the people who did the actual ferrying of goods across from mainland Europe were highly skilled mariners in need of extra cash. Ex-soldiers and sailors sometimes took up smuggling, especially when there was a break in whatever war was going on, when many of them would find themselves without work.

Small sailing ships, sleekly designed for speed, would scoot across the English Channel in the dead of night and flash a light towards land. If they were answered by a light, they'd move in closer and start unloading. Locals would be hired as 'tubmen' (to fetch and carry the smuggled goods), or as 'batsmen' (literally armed with a wooden bat, to deal with any trouble).

There are many legends of smugglers hiding their loot in coastal caves, or in specially-dug tunnels. Such stories are almost all untrue. However, smugglers did devise many devious ways to hide goods from the authorities.

Four ingenious methods smugglers used to hide stuff

1. They'd conceal it in places where few self-respecting officials would care to look, such as in graveyards and tombs.

2. They'd bury it under sandy beaches, taking care to record its exact position. A few gusts of wind, and nobody could tell the sand had even been disturbed.

3. They'd tie boxes or barrels together into a raft, then weigh it all down just enough for the raft to duck under the surface of the sea. The raft could float into shore, all but invisible.

4. If they suspected an ambush on shore, they'd throw boxes overboard and let them sink, leaving a long string topped with a feather. The feather would float, marking the location, ready for the boxes to be collected later using a hook on a rope.

With enormous quantities of goods being sneaked across the coasts every year, you'd think there'd have been a small army of highly trained officers bringing smugglers to justice. But not a bit of it. For the most part, those whose job it was to police the coastline were few in number and often willing to turn a blind eye.

There'd been Riding Officers – officials on horseback who would patrol at irregular times and places to catch the smugglers out – since 1698. But there were nowhere near enough of them to keep an eye on everything, and the threat of violence was usually enough to send them packing. Besides, they were stuck on land. All the smugglers had to do, if they got wind of a Riding Officer, was to sail away again.

Things didn't improve even when the Riding Officers could call on the army for help. In any case, officials who tried to stop the smuggling – customs officials – were part of their local communities too. Although the job paid well (if they actually recovered any smuggled goods), being one of the King's Men made them so unpopular in the neighbourhood that it was preferable to let the smugglers do what they liked.

As the problem got worse (because the taxes kept getting higher, meaning the smugglers could make more money, so more people turned to smuggling), the good guys and the bad guys ended up in an endless cat-and-mouse chase. The government's reaction was to pass even more laws and make the penalties for smuggling very severe (you could be transported to the other side of the world just for resisting arrest).

As a consequence, smuggling became a very violent occupation. Smugglers would kill customs officers, or each other, or anyone who informed on them, to avoid being caught.

Smuggling reached a peak in the early nineteenth century. In 1815, the Royal Navy was brought in to try to defeat the smugglers, and by blocking routes across the Channel over the next two years they seized over nine hundred illegal shipments.

It was 1831 before a permanent and effective coastguard service was established, but by then smuggling was on the way out anyway. Why? For the simple reason that all those taxes were beginning to be replaced by trade agreements with other countries. In the 1840s, Britain changed to a policy of free trade with most of the world and the market for smuggled goods all but vanished.

Something which had been a major problem for well over a century now just melted away! Smuggling is a perfect example of how politics and economics have an enormous influence on crime and on its detection and policing.

HIGHWAYMEN

A highwayman was someone on horseback who robbed travellers, as opposed to a 'footpad', who was someone on foot who robbed travellers. In the American Wild West, such robbers were called 'road agents', and in Australia they were known as 'bushrangers'.

There are a lot of myths and misconceptions surrounding highwaymen. The image of the highwayman as a dashing, masked and cloaked figure, being charming to the ladies while collecting up jewels in a leather purse, is totally fictional. One or two well-known highwaymen had a reputation for stealing politely, but the vast majority of them were nothing more than a bunch of vicious thugs. Although, oddly enough, they really did say things like 'Stand and deliver!' and 'Your money or your life!' (Such phrases are listed in trial records from that time.)

So where does this romanticised version come from? Mostly, it's down to what various authors wrote about various highwaymen after those highwaymen were caught, hanged and long gone. We'll come back to this in a minute.

The heyday of the highwayman lasted from late Elizabethan times to the early nineteenth century but it was at its worst in the eighteenth century. Horse-drawn coaches made prime targets, as did anyone using main routes across the country such as the Great North Road which went from London to York and beyond, or the Great Dover Road going south-east from the capital. For years, the single most dangerous place to travel in England was Hounslow Heath (which occupied roughly the same area as Heathrow Airport does today) where several major roads crossed.

The penalty for robbery with violence was hanging, and that's how almost all highwaymen ended up. Most of them barely made it into their twenties, what with the dangers of a life on the run and so many fellow crooks willing to turn them in to the authorities for cash.

The most famous highwayman of them all is Dick

Turpin. He really did exist, but he was nothing like his later legend suggests.

Turpin was an Essex lad, born in 1705. He was a butcher in Whitechapel, which today is right in the middle of London, but was then a village on the outskirts of the city. Instead of buying meat for his shop, he used to steal sheep and cattle from surrounding farms.

Once his little scheme was rumbled (it didn't exactly take long for farmers to work out where their missing cattle were ending up!), he turned to smuggling. He was equally bad at that and was soon on the run from the customs officials. Then he spent a long period as part of a gang, which specialised in raiding remote farmhouses, as well as highway robbery.

Turpin's gang became notorious for ruthlessness and brutality. They caused so much trouble that King George II offered a fifty-pound reward for their capture (equal to over £50,000 today!).

His exploits regularly made the papers, but Dick Turpin was still, as you might say, a long way from being the sharpest tool in the box. One good example: he stole a particularly fine horse one night from a Mr Major. Major was so angry that he decided to track Turpin down himself. He toured the pubs of London handing out leaflets about the theft, and the horse was quickly identified as being stabled at the Red Lion pub in Whitechapel. Major and some local officers hid at the stable and pounced on Turpin's accomplice when he came to collect the horse. Turpin himself, who arrived just after, rode towards the officers at top speed, firing pistols at them. But he was such a bad shot that all he hit was his accomplice!

This incident marked the beginning of the end for Turpin. His accomplice died, but not before he'd given the authorities enough information to trap Turpin. Well, you would if you'd been shot like that, wouldn't you!

Turpin fled to York and adopted the name John Palmer. Even then, he might have escaped justice, if only he hadn't written to his brother back in London asking him to get rid of any remaining evidence. Turpin's brother was too mean to pay the postage and the letter ended up being opened at the post office. Turpin had written down more than enough to get himself caught. He was hanged in 1739 and his grave can be seen in the churchyard of St Denys & St George in York.

The myth of the dashing highwayman started up almost immediately when the completely inaccurate *Life of Richard Turpin* was published just after his execution. However, it was almost a century later, in 1834, when a novel called *Rookwood* by Harrison Ainsworth turned Turpin's life into the fiction we know today.

The general public in 1834 was perfectly happy to think of highwaymen as heroic figures, despite what they did. It was mostly rich people who were robbed, so the vast majority of poor citizens enjoyed a good laugh at any toff's misfortune.

Also, by that time, highway robbery was becoming a thing of the past. The expansion of railways, increased used of toll roads and the beginnings of an efficient police system (see page 104) all made getaways very difficult for a robber on horseback. The last recorded robbery by a highwayman was reported in 1831.

THE WORLD'S FIRST GANSTER? JONATHAN WILD

During the second half of the seventeenth century, London was suffering from increasing levels of crime as the population of the city rose and the proportion of relatively well-off people grew.

A system of 'thief-takers' was established in the early years of the eighteenth century (for more information, see the section 'In the Years BC (Before Cops)' on page 102). The most notorious of these was a man called Jonathan Wild.

He'd been born into a poor family in Wolverhampton in about 1682 or 1683 (it's not known exactly when). Once he got fed up of being an apprentice buckle-maker, he moved to London, but by 1710 had landed himself in debtors' prison.

There, he quickly learnt about the workings of the city's criminal underworld. As soon as he was free, he and his new girlfriend Mary started trading in stolen goods. In 1713, the first London thief-taker, Charles Hitchin, who was himself no stranger to crime and corruption, recruited Wild as an assistant. This was how Jonathan Wild began the most scandalous public career of the 1700s.

He set up his official thief-taker's office in Newtoner's Lane. Here, anyone who'd had something stolen could come and ask for his help in getting their stuff back and – for an extra fee – bring those responsible to justice.

He was immensely successful at reuniting people with their stolen items. To ordinary Londoners, he was a hero, helping to clean up the streets.

What the law-abiding majority didn't know was that Jonathan Wild was using his position as thief-taker to create a criminal empire. The basic scam went like this: Wild had many connections in the underworld and with penalties for theft being so severe at the time (execution, generally), it made sense for thieves to bring everything they'd stolen to him. He would then pay them a percentage of their worth. Then the true owners would arrive asking for help. Never fear, says

Wild, I'm sure we can track your possessions down and, lo and behold, here they are. That'll be a few shillings, please.

This con was so successful that Wild had people stealing goods to order, just so the owners would then come running to Wild and beg for his 'services'. Pretty soon, Wild was amassing a sizeable pile of cash through this city-wide steal-and-sell trick.

Wild dominated all criminal activity. He could use his official status as thief-taker to remove any gangs or individuals who got in his way or did anything he didn't like. If any member of his network double-crossed him or worked for a rival criminal, he would have them captured and imprisoned (or worse) on any thin or bogus charge he might think up. And he'd get well paid by the government for every thief he 'took'!

For years, he ran a variety of specialist gangs: one for robbing churches, one for house breaking, and so on. He even had his own boat for smuggling goods into and out of mainland Europe. Wild himself kept well away from the actual crimes and presented a heroic, gang-busting image to the authorities. And all the time, as a thief-taker, he could protect his own followers from justice and have opponents silenced.

Jonathan Wild's criminal network was what today we'd call 'organised crime'. And like so many gangsters, he was finally brought down by a few small details which spiralled out of control.

In 1725, Wild got caught up in a complicated squabble with Jack Sheppard, a notorious robber. Sheppard had worked for Wild at one time, but was now trying to go it alone. There was no way, of course, Wild would put up with that.

Wild had Sheppard arrested – several times, because Sheppard was a master at escaping from jail! As events dragged in more of Wild's network, suspicion began to fall on Wild himself, and when angry gang members started to inform on each other, Wild's entire organisation began to crumble. He was arrested, the public discovered the truth about him, and there was absolute outrage throughout the city. His situation was made all the worse by the fact that the public had recently learnt of various political scandals and was in no mood to tolerate someone as corrupt as Jonathan Wild.

Tickets were sold for his execution, scheduled for May 24th 1725. Wild was so scared he tried all kinds of excuses to avoid the hangman, but to no avail. His body ended up being used for study by doctors, and his skeleton was put on display in the museum of the Royal College of Surgeons in London – and it's still there!

Jonathan Wild was so famous a crook that he inspired a

long string of fictional works and literary 're-enactments'. For instance, Daniel Defoe, the author of *Robinson Crusoe*, wrote a book called *A True and Genuine Account of the Life and Actions of the Late Jonathan Wild* – bit of a mouthful! Threads of the Wild story can be traced through quite a few later works too, including one of the Sherlock Holmes stories (Wild is mentioned by name in *The Valley of Fear*).

It can be argued that, since Jonathan Wild was the first example of what you'd call an organised crime boss, all the gangster stories of modern times owe something to him!

GRAVE ROBBERS
AND
BODY SNATCHERS

For a period of about eighty years, from the mid-1700s up to 1832, there was a constant and almost unstoppable trade in dead human bodies. The idea of grave robbing is an ancient one – look at what happened to all those Egyptian pharaohs' tombs! – but the difference here was that the robbers weren't usually interested in stealing jewellery or other artefacts. It was the corpses they wanted.

Why? Several factors criss-crossed to create the grisly occupation of what were often called 'resurrection men'.

Scientific and medical knowledge was growing. More people were being trained as doctors and part of medical training is the study of human anatomy. Students needed real bodies to examine in order to learn about how the body works.

By the end of the 1700s, fewer people were being condemned to death by the law courts. The punishment for trivial crimes – nicking an apple, say – gradually became less extreme. A fine, instead of execution, for instance! Since medical students relied on executed criminals for their supply of bodies, this caused a shortage.

The Industrial Revolution caused a big increase in the number of people living in towns and cities. Large numbers of these people were very poor. When poverty drove them to consider a life of crime, body snatching was an attractive choice, despite how horrific it was.

What's the Difference?

A **grave robber** is someone who digs up an already-buried dead body and runs off with it. A **body snatcher** is someone who steals, or tricks their way into getting hold of, a dead body which hasn't been buried.

Body snatching was an almost totally British problem – there was a similar trade going on in some parts of America, at around the same time, but it was almost unheard of across the rest of Europe. This was because, in Britain at that time, people did not want to donate their bodies to medical research when they died – there were a number of taboos and superstitions surrounding the cutting up of bodies, mainly based on the religious beliefs of the time. On top of that, the fact that corpses of executed criminals were given to medical students led to the view that any other dead body used in this way was no better than that of the worst thief or murderer. In 1752, parliament passed a law which said that *anyone* convicted of murder would have their body given over for dissection (cutting up). Result: even more public horror at any non-criminal giving their body up for dissection.

Throughout the second half of the eighteenth century, it was common to see fights over a corpse breaking out at the scene of executions. The friends and relatives of an executed criminal would literally have to defend their dead loved ones against a mob of people (including medical students) wanting to take the body.

Selling bodies to medical schools was a good way to make money: first, because the medical schools paid well for each body, and second, because the penalty if you were caught was minimal. If you stole a ring off a dead body, you could be hanged (and end up dissected yourself!). If you stole *only* the corpse, you'd probably get little more than a slap on the wrist. Possessions were considered more valuable than people!

Price List

An average adult corpse would earn you about £4 (equal to over £200 in today's money). Prices rose to around £10 by the 1830s. Children ('smalls') were bought by length – you got more the taller they'd grown. Teeth were bought by dentists, who used them to make dentures.

It became common for the body of anyone at all who died to be watched over by their family, in case body snatchers turned up. Sometimes, metal cages were fixed over graves to prevent them being dug up.

In response, body snatchers developed lots of devious tricks. They'd turn up at workhouses, weeping and wailing, to claim the body of their dear, dear, recently departed friend, er, we'll have that one over there, before those *awful* body snatchers got to 'em. They'd attend funerals in order to spot any problems they might have when they raided the grave later. A favourite ploy was to bribe the servants of richer folk – the servants would replace the body in the coffin with something heavy, before the burial took place.

All too often, body snatchers got away with it simply because the authorities turned a blind eye. After all, the country needed doctors and doctors needed bodies. Workhouses were perfectly happy to have unclaimed corpses snatched – it saved the cost of dealing with them themselves. It even got to the point where medical students could (on the quiet!) pay part of their tuition fees in dead bodies.

How to Rob a Grave

The standard method for grave-robbing in the 1700s was to work in a small gang. Late at night, by only a thin shaft of light from a covered lamp, a hole would be dug at the head-end of the grave. Only wooden spades would be used, since these made less noise that metal ones, especially if they hit a stone. Once the top of the coffin was found, its lid would be broken open (using a hook or crowbar levered against the weight of earth on the rest of the coffin lid). A rope would be tied around the body and it would be hauled out. Any clothes or valuables would be thrown back (to avoid a harsh punishment if caught). Then the hole would be carefully refilled and made to look undisturbed. Experienced gangs could do all this in less than an hour.

Body snatching was effectively ended by the Anatomy Act of 1832. This regulated the medical schools, and also put tight controls on what could or could not happen to human corpses. At long last, there could be a balance between the needs of medical research and the treatment of the dead.

Just as changes in the law more or less put a stop to smuggling (see page 15), so body snatching and grave robbing in Britain was – pardon the pun! – stopped dead in its tracks after 1832.

THE KING OF CAT BURGLARS
CHARLES PEACE

Near the beginning of the Sherlock Holmes story *The Adventure of the Illustrious Client,* Holmes is talking with a visitor to his rooms at 221B Baker Street:

'A complex mind,' said Holmes. 'All great criminals have that. My old friend Charlie Peace was a violin virtuoso.'

There really was a famous Victorian criminal called Charles Peace, and he really was an accomplished musician. He was also sometimes called 'King of Cat Burglars' – he broke into buildings in a particularly stealthy and silent way and became notorious in the latter years of the nineteenth century as both a thief and a murderer.

Accident

In 1846, when he was 14, Peace was involved in an accident while working at a steel mill. A shard of red hot metal entered his leg just below the knee and he spent over a year in a Sheffield infirmary. His later burglaries are all the more remarkable since his leg was badly damaged for the rest of his life!

It's thought that his earliest crime was the stealing of an old man's gold pocket watch, sometime around 1850. By the following year he was breaking into the homes of wealthy folk in his home town of Sheffield. He was soon caught, when some of the items he stole were found in his possession.

For years, he was in and out of one prison after another. No sooner was he released than he went back to thieving and got himself locked up again. He made an unsuccessful escape attempt in 1864, using a saw he'd made himself out of a piece of tin.

After he was released in 1872, he (and, on and off, his wife) drifted around various parts of northern England. He committed his first murder in 1876, shooting a police constable who intercepted him as he tried to make a getaway from one of his burglaries. Two brothers, John and William Harbon, were wrongly accused of the killing. John was acquitted (declared not guilty) but William was sentenced to life in prison. Charles Peace was sitting in the public gallery of the court during the whole trial.

Jack of all Trades

Apart from being a violin player and steel worker, Charles Peace tried his hand at a number of other jobs, including being an 'eating-shop' owner, a picture frame maker (the tools proved very useful for burglary!) and an inventor – he designed, among other things, a smoke helmet for firemen and a special brush for washing railway carriages!

Shortly after this, Peace shot another man, a friend of his called Dyson. He'd been bullying both Mr and Mrs Dyson for ages, and the understandable fuss kicked up by Mrs Dyson after the shooting made Peace a fugitive from the law. A £100 reward was offered for him, dead or alive, and police across the north-east circulated his details:

'Charles Peace, wanted for Murder on the night of 29th inst. He is thin and slightly built, from fifty-five to sixty years of age. Five feet four inches or five feet high; grey (nearly white) hair, beard and whiskers, he lacks use of three fingers, walks

with his legs rather wide apart, speaks somewhat peculiarly as though his tongue were too large for his mouth, and is a great boaster . . .'

He sounds freakish! They were wrong, however – Peace was only 44. Those useless fingers were the result of his mishandling a gun, after which he took to wearing a metal plate on his hand with a hook attached to it.

Charles Peace managed to avoid capture, partly through his cat burgling ability to clamber around the outside of buildings undetected, and partly by changing his appearance as far as he could: he shaved, dyed his hair, put on spectacles and could twist his face in such a way that he'd appear to be much older.

He continued moving around the country – and continually stealing – with police forces on the lookout for him and further rewards being offered for his capture.

It was after he arrived in London in 1877 that he started to become well-known by the public. For about two years, he robbed homes all over the city and beyond, embarrassing Scotland Yard and whipping the newspapers into a frenzy of headlines. Every night, he'd prowl the darkened streets looking for likely targets.

He was finally cornered in the early hours of October 10th 1878. Constable Robinson of Scotland Yard saw a suspicious light in the window of a house in Blackheath.

He alerted two other officers to ring the bell at the front of the house, while he stayed at the back, in the garden.

As soon as the doorbell rang, Robinson spotted a figure slinking from the dining room window. He followed; Charles Peace turned and cried, 'Keep back! Or by God I'll shoot you!' And shoot he did, five times, although Robinson managed to escape serious injury. The other officers arrived and Peace's reign as King of the Cat Burglars was over.

Scotland Yard began to piece together the full picture of Peace's life and crimes, helped by various people Peace had crossed over the years. It was soon apparent that William Habron was innocent, and Peace was moved north to stand trial. He made a last-minute escape attempt, by jumping through the open window of a moving train, but he was so badly beaten up by the leap that he was simply picked up by the next train along the line!

Charles Peace was executed in February 1879. It's said that he ate a hearty breakfast that morning, but complained about the quality of the bacon.

JACK THE RIPPER

The mystery of Jack the Ripper is perhaps the most famous criminal case in history and to this day remains unsolved. So much time having passed, and so many conflicting clues and theories having clouded the investigation, it's unlikely it will ever be solved.

The East End of London was a grim place in 1888. Thousands of very poor, sometimes starving, people were crammed into filthy, cramped buildings, which lined the narrow and even filthier streets. The Whitechapel district, where the murders occurred, displayed all the worst aspects of Victorian life and Victorian attitudes. Much of it was a no-go area as far as the police were concerned.

The case of Jack the Ripper is such an astonishingly large and complex one that this book would need to be several hundred pages long just to list all the facts! Some interesting aspects of the case are:

1. Five horribly gruesome murders are generally attributed to Jack the Ripper, although there were eleven in the period between 1888 and 1891 which some have argued were connected.

2. The five murders are linked because they share what's called a *modus operandi* (m.o.) – the criminal used very similar methods and equipment to commit the crime and/or targeted similar people in a similar location or at a similar time of day.

3. Police files from the time give us a detailed insight into how they conducted the investigation. Over 2000 people were interviewed; over 300 were investigated in more detail; 80 were arrested on suspicion.

4. Some of the many, many people suspected of being the Ripper over the years include butchers, surgeons, various Members of Parliament, Queen

Victoria's son Prince Albert Victor (and her doctor Sir William Gull), several Whitechapel tradesmen, an assistant at the local morgue and the artist Walter Sickert. It's also been argued that the murders were done by a woman. There was even a totally wild theory that Lewis Carroll, author of *Alice in Wonderland*, was the killer!

5. The investigation included a very early example of what we would now call 'criminal profiling': trying to work out what sort of person the criminal is, what sort of job they do, what their everyday life is like and so on, all based on how the crime has been committed.

6. The nickname Jack the Ripper is taken from one of the gloating letters, apparently written by the killer, sent to the police and the newspapers. It's not known how many, if any, of these letters were genuine. Until that letter was published, the killer was referred to as 'Leather Apron'.

7. The police investigation was led by Detective Inspector Edmund Reid, although it's Scotland Yard's Inspector Frederick Abbeline whose name is most often associated with the case.

8. People living in the East End got so fed up with the lack of progress on the case that a group of volunteers formed the Whitechapel Vigilance Committee. They patrolled the streets looking for suspicious characters, asked parliament to put up a reward for the killer's capture and hired private detectives to question witnesses.

If you want to read more about Jack the Ripper, you'll have no trouble at all finding information. Be warned: it's truly the stuff of nightmares!

PUBLIC ENEMY
NUMBER ONE

In the early years of the twentieth century, the crime rate in America was on the rise.

1929 was a disastrous year for the American economy, and for the economies of most of the Western world, following a huge crash on the stock market. (Stock market crashes are mind-bogglingly complicated things – just assume it means lots of people losing their jobs, lots of poverty, lots of businesses going bust, that sort of thing. Crashes happen now and again even today, but 1929's was the worst ever.) The Wall Street Crash led directly to the Great Depression, a period in the 1930s during which most Americans lost their jobs and became very poor.

Out of the already gangster-ridden streets of America's cities came more criminals. Bonnie and Clyde were an example of this new wave (see page 54).

Criminal and . . . Hero?

Just like the English highwaymen of the 1700s (see page 16), American crooks of the '30s were often bizarrely popular figures, and for the same reason: at a time when vast numbers of people lived in terrible poverty, anyone who robbed banks and generally thumbed their noses at authority might be secretly admired. Lots of gangster movies based on real-life events were made, and this was the period in which Hardboiled detective fiction was at its height (see page 183).

America's FBI was just getting started, as the Bureau of Investigations – for more information on FBI history, see page 116 – and federal agents were often stretched to the limit by one notorious villain after another. The period 1931-1935 has sometimes been called the 'era of public enemies', because of the sheer number of large-scale crooks who found themselves on official Most Wanted lists. It almost became a badge of honour to be labelled 'Public Enemy Number One'!

The worst-affected area in America was the north-east

which was plagued by crooks such as Al Capone, 'Pretty Boy' Floyd, Kate 'Ma' Barker and 'Machine Gun' Kelly.

The city of Chicago was a particular focus for criminal activity, partly because it was a very large place, which contained a lot of places to hide out, and plenty of ready-to-rob banks.

Weapon of Choice

The public enemies had an advantage over the law enforcers. The sub-machine gun had been developed as a weapon during World War I, and was meant for the US army, but it was taken up by gangsters because it was light, compact and deadly. The police mostly had pistols.

The inter-connected stories of two crooks who got to the Number One slot on the Public Enemy list, 'Baby Face' Nelson and John Dillinger, are a good example of what the police faced, and the miserable end that most of these villains came to.

Nelson, whose real name was Lester Gillis, had been in and out of trouble all his life. He took to armed robbery like a duck to water. He got his nickname after he robbed the mayor of Chicago's wife in 1930 and she told the police that 'he had a baby face . . . hardly more than a boy'. In fact, he was twenty-two at the time, but his short stature and his facial features always made him look younger.

Nelson was a particularly nasty character who never hesitated to shoot to kill. Weirdly, he was also a family man who even dragged his wife and kids around with him when he was on the run from the law!

Nelson's gang committed a long series of bank robberies and in 1934 they're thought to have been involved in John Dillinger's dramatic escape from prison.

Like Nelson, Dillinger had been a petty crook since childhood, stealing cars as a teenager and spending several years in jail for robbing a grocery store. Also like Nelson, he'd been part of a gang. One of Dillinger's favourite tricks was to find out about the weak points of a bank's security while posing as a burglar alarm salesman – he'd walk in, offer his 'services', and be told all about their security! Other times, the gang would pose as film-makers shooting a bank robbery scene – people would stand around watching the action, not realising that the bank robbery they were witnessing was for real!

Dillinger and his gang were arrested in early 1934, after they were recognised from pictures in a magazine called *True Detective*. Police boasted that their jail was escape-proof but posted extra guards just to be sure. Dillinger secretly carved a fake gun from a piece of wood, and promptly used it to threaten his way through when he broke out!

It was at this point that Dillinger and 'Baby Face' Nelson's gang joined forces. However, the Bureau of Investigations was hot on their trail.

When the gang took refuge at the secluded Little Bohemia Lodge, a holiday hideaway in the countryside, the Bureau had a perfect opportunity to sneak up and catch them unaware. But the whole operation, under the command of federal agent Melvin Purvis, was badly bungled. Several innocent bystanders were killed.

Although the gang members escaped, this event marked the beginning of the end for every last one of them. The Bureau was heavily criticised for its mistake, and agents were determined to bring Nelson, Dillinger and the others to justice.

Over the following weeks, one gang member after another was tracked down. Some were arrested, some shot dead while trying to escape.

John Dillinger met his end in July 1934. A Romanian immigrant to the US, Anna Sage, agreed to help the police catch him in return for staying in the country. She arranged to go with Dillinger to a cinema in Chicago, wearing a brightly coloured dress so that the Bureau agents could easily identify her in the dim light from the screen.

Once agents had confirmed that Dillinger was with Anna Sage, they waited silently outside (rather than risk a gun battle in a crowded cinema). The movie being shown was, believe it or not, a gangster film, *Manhattan Melodrama* starring Clark Gable and Myrna Loy, two of the biggest Hollywood stars of the time.

As the crowd left the cinema, Melvin Purvis signalled to his fellow agents and Dillinger was hit by three bullets and killed. Newspapers later reported that passers-by, discovering what had happened, started dipping handkerchiefs in Dillinger's blood, as a souvenir!

'Baby Face' Nelson's career in crime ended that November, after spending months running from place to place across America. Two federal agents driving near Chicago spotted Nelson and his wife driving past them in the opposite direction.

Nelson recognised the agents at the same moment. After a series of screeching u-turns, Nelson managed to shoot out the windscreen of the agents' car, which then swerved violently to avoid an oncoming truck and ended up in a field. The agents, knowing Nelson's brutal reputation, feared that he'd come back for revenge.

However, unknown to them, two more federal agents had taken up the chase. Nelson's car had been damaged by gunfire and it skidded to a halt at a nearby petrol station. There was a gun battle in which both the agents were shot dead. Nelson had been shot nine times and although he and his wife fled using the agents' car, he died later that day.

SCARFACE
AND
THE UNTOUCHABLES

In 1920, a new law was passed in America which banned the making and selling of alcohol. The crime rate had been rising and it was thought that this law – 'Prohibition' as it was called – would help tackle a range of social problems such as crime.

It didn't. Prohibition was not only unpopular with the American public, it was a law they were prepared to ignore. The 1920s in the States became known as the Jazz Age, a time of music, dance, youth, style and daring fashions. So Prohibition was a bit of a party pooper.

A huge, illegal trade was created almost overnight. In every city, criminal gangs and gangsters started charging eye-popping prices for cheaply-produced alcoholic drinks (some of which were almost literally poison – but complain? No way!) and alcohol was smuggled in from abroad. Illegal nightclubs known as 'speakeasys' appeared in many places, tucked away in backstreets or otherwise hidden from public view. The gangsters had always sunk their claws in all kinds of criminal activities, but the profits of Prohibition enabled them to create powerful, localised crime empires, which they defended violently.

The most famous of these gangsters, even to this day, was Chicago's Al Capone (pronounced Cap-own). He was born in New York in 1899, was expelled from school at the age of fourteen and moved to Chicago in 1920 to be chief henchman to a crime boss called Johnny Torrio.

Nickname

Capone got his nickname, 'Scarface', after an incident during his teenage years in New York. He got into a fight and was badly cut on the left side of his face. For the rest of his life, Capone tried to hide his scars when photographed and often claimed they were war wounds.

Capone was disgustingly successful at beating off Torrio's rival gangsters, often literally. If they wouldn't take the hint, he'd simply murder them. When Torrio was badly injured by enemies in 1925, he decided to retire to Italy and handed over his 'business' to Al Capone.

Even before he took over Chicago's criminal underworld, Capone had become an expert at bribery and corruption. He would pay police and politicians to turn a blind eye, and his thugs would hang around polling stations at election times to intimidate people into voting for Capone's candidates. It's estimated he spent a grand total of $75 million on bribes.

By the late 1920s, Al Capone's organisation had a vice-like grip on the city. He had a public profile as high as any celebrity's, and a lifestyle as luxurious as royalty. He established his headquarters in the elegant (and very expensive) Lexington Hotel, all the time describing himself on his business card as simply a 'used-furniture dealer'.

Hey Yooz Mugs!

Al Capone is the person most of the stereotyped American gangsters of film and fiction are based on. Any old-fashioned fictional gangster you come across with a wide-brimmed hat, overcoat and heavy 'Noo Yoik' accent is basically Capone. So is the casual 'Hey, I'm just a businessman' attitude you find in such characters.

Capone's bitterest enemies were Hymie Weiss and 'Bugs' Moran, rival Chicago mob bosses. The gangs fought violently for territory – more than two hundred gangsters were killed over a four-year period. They tried to kill Capone himself several times and he soon took to travelling everywhere in a bullet-proof Cadillac. And so did his bodyguards.

On February 14th 1929, Capone arranged for seven rivals (including Moran) to be shot dead in what became known as the St Valentine's Day Massacre. Although this eliminated some of the competition, it also caused widespread outrage amongst the public.

US President Herbert Hoover demanded action. Special investigation squads were set up to specifically target Capone's mob. One of these squads was led by a Bureau of Prohibition agent called Eliot Ness, a man whose name would become associated with tough, no-nonsense crime fighting for decades to come.

Ness realised that if he was going to fight Capone, he would need to have a team he could trust. This was much harder than it sounded because huge numbers of police and other officials had been bribed (or threatened) by Capone's organisation.

Ness combed through the personnel records of every agent available, looking for those without the slightest hint of corruption. In the end, he was down to just nine men. Ness and these agents stood alone against the entire Capone mob, numbered in the hundreds.

Naturally, Capone tried to bribe Ness's men too. However, Ness and his team called a press conference and made it all public, to show people that they were honest and trustworthy and that they were dedicated to ending Capone's hold on Chicago. The media were so impressed that Ness and his team were instantly dubbed 'The Untouchables'.

As you might expect, after that Capone tried to have Ness and his men killed several times. On one occasion, Eliot Ness noticed, purely by chance, that the bonnet of his car had been opened: he narrowly avoided setting off a bomb that had been placed in the engine!

Piece by piece, The Untouchables chipped away at Capone's crime empire, raiding breweries and gradually reducing the supplies of alcohol that Capone's organisation needed to maintain its profits.

Ness sometimes used clever psychological tactics in his war against Capone. For instance, after a while The Untouchables had seized as many as forty of Capone's transport trucks. To demonstrate that he was getting results, Ness had all of them driven slowly past Capone's HQ at the Lexington Hotel one morning. Capone, watching from his window, was utterly furious, and utterly unable to do anything about it.

Quite a lot of the information which The Untouchables used to intercept shipments or raid warehouses came from wire tapping (secretly listening in to phone lines). In places where they couldn't physically place a wire tap on the crooks' telephones – no mobiles in those days, don't forget! – they would resort to trickery. One of Capone's offices, an important target, had phone wires Ness's men couldn't get to. They sent an undercover agent into the office, to tell the crooks that the place would soon be raided by The Untouchables, so Capone's mob moved offices to somewhere Ness could more easily place a tap!

It was this sort of detailed info-gathering which finally brought Al Capone down. Did they arrest him for breaking Prohibition? Robbery? Murder? No – it was for not paying his taxes.

Capone, who for so many years had felt he was beyond the reach of the law, was caught out because he hadn't filled in a tax form for a long time. Once Ness could prove that Capone clearly had a very, very large income, and yet had paid no tax, the gangster's days of freedom were numbered. In 1931, Al Capone was arrested on twenty-two counts of tax evasion, totalling over $200,000 – over $3 million in today's money.

Capone was convicted despite a last-minute attempt to bribe the trial jury. He was escorted to prison on a train manned by Eliot Ness and the rest of The Untouchables.

BONNIE AND CLYDE

In January 1930, in Dallas, Texas, two young people met at the house of a mutual friend. It was pretty much love at first sight.

Bonnie Parker was a short, rather scrawny nineteen-year-old. She'd been working as a waitress, but now that the Great Depression was biting (see *Public Enemy Number One*, page 41), she was out of work. She was also married to a man who was in jail for armed robbery.

Clyde Barrow was twenty-one, a fast-talking small-time thief who had little idea of what to do with his life except to 'be somebody'. A couple of weeks after the two of them met, Barrow was sentenced to two years in prison for a number of previous crimes.

He ended up in the notoriously brutal Eastham Prison Farm in Texas, where prisoners had to spend their days doing various forms of hard manual work. Barrow hated the place. He tried to get out of work by having one of the other convicts chop two of his toes off! The trick didn't work, and Barrow left prison in 1932 on crutches.

Prison had been so horrible that he vowed never to end up there again. It didn't seem to occur to him that the best way to do that would be to stop committing crimes!

It was clear that Barrow would be living life on the run from now on, and that things were highly unlikely to end happily ever after. Even so, Bonnie Parker went along with him.

For the next two years, the Barrow Gang robbed and shot their way across the southern American states of Texas, Oklahoma, Missouri, Louisiana and New Mexico. For most of that time, Clyde's older brother Ivan, known as Buck, and Buck's wife Blanche, were also part of the gang. Several other gang members came and went at various times, too.

The Barrow Gang moved swiftly from state to state, taking advantage of the fact that, at the time, police from one US state couldn't arrest someone in another state. The cops would have to give up the chase if it crossed the border (or 'state line'). Barrow was also an expert driver, who studied maps to gain an encyclopedic knowledge of every tiny back road, which might be useful for getaways.

When compared to many well-known criminals, Barrow, Parker and co. were distinctly unsuccessful: they often robbed small grocery stores and petrol stations, and even when they robbed banks they rarely got away with much money. They lived in their (stolen) cars most of the time, never had much cash and were always fearful of being caught. They were also ruthless and brutal – between them, they shot dead well over ten people.

A scratch-a-living gang of thugs like that might easily have been forgotten by history, but instead they achieved enormous fame right across the country. Their crimes were front-page news everywhere, to such an extent that they were blamed for lots of crimes they didn't actually commit.

The American public saw Bonnie and Clyde as a sort of Romeo and Juliet with machine guns, a young couple in love running from the clutches of authority. How could they have got such a muddled impression? The Barrow Gang certainly acted as if they were off on some sort of wild adventure: a favourite trick was to let a police car catch up with them and then they'd kidnap the cops inside. They would drive around for a few hours and then dump the cops in the middle of nowhere, miles from home.

What created Barrow and Parker's twisted-Robin-Hood image more than anything else was something that happened in April 1933. The police tracked the gang to a rented flat in Joplin, Missouri. There was a fierce gun battle and several cops were hurt, but the gang all escaped.

However, they'd left all their stuff behind them. Amongst what the police found was a roll of film, containing photos of Bonnie and Clyde posing and smiling. They also found a sentimental poem, written by Bonnie Parker, entitled *The Story of Suicide Sal*. The pictures and poem appeared in newspapers, creating – along with the story of their dramatic escape – an image of two glamorous, slightly tragic young outlaws.

Meanwhile, the gang were almost cut to pieces in another police raid. Buck Barrow died of gunshot wounds, and Blanche was captured. Bonnie and Clyde barely escaped alive.

The following November, another of the gang, W. D. Jones, was captured and questioned. For the first time, police learnt one very important fact: both Barrow and Parker made frequent trips back into Texas to see their families.

Police were positioned close to the families' homes. Once more, Barrow and Parker escaped, but not before the lives of both their mothers had been put in danger. Barrow in particular was furious.

Clyde Barrow decided on revenge. The Barrow Gang attacked the Eastham Prison Farm, where Clyde had been locked up, and managed to free a number of inmates.

For the authorities in Texas, this was the last straw. They hired a bounty hunter and ex-Texas Ranger called Frank Hamer. He was a tall, gritty lawman, like something out of the Wild West, and he had a reputation for shooting first and asking questions later. He was given the job of heading a team to hunt down the Barrow Gang.

One of the prisoners freed from Eastham was a young man called Henry Methvin. He rode along with the Barrow Gang for a while, but soon became alarmed at Bonnie and Clyde's fatalistic attitude: they took it for granted that they'd end their days in a police shoot-out. Methvin wanted to live.

When Bonnie and Clyde took refuge for a while at Methvin's father house in Louisiana, Henry confided his fears to his dad. His father secretly went to the police, and agreed to supply information in return for a reduced prison sentence for Henry.

Frank Hamer spotted an opportunity for an ambush. Bonnie and Clyde were now driving around in a brand new tan-coloured Ford V8 Sedan, a very distinctive car. Henry's father said that the pair of them drove into the nearest town almost every day.

Hamer placed Henry's father's battered old truck along the road out of town, making it look as if the vehicle had broken down. He guessed correctly that when Clyde drove past, he'd see the truck and stop to help.

The road was surrounded by trees and thick bushes, a perfect place for Hamer's team to lie in wait. At just after 9 o'clock in the morning on May 23rd 1934, the Ford V8 glided to a stop beside the truck.

Hamer was well aware that Bonnie and Clyde had escaped similar situations several times. He was determined to make sure it didn't happen again. As the car came to a stop, six police officers stepped quickly out of the bushes and fired over a hundred times, killing them both.

One of the officers present later wrote that, *a drumbeat of shells knifes through the steel body of the car, and glass is shattering . . . [When the firing stops] I scramble over the hood of the car and throw open the door on Bonnie's side . . . I smell a light perfume against the burned-cordite smell of gunpowder.*

Here's a shortened version of Bonnie Parker's (not very good) poem *The Ballad of Bonnie and Clyde*, or *The Trail's End*, which Parker's mother got published in newspapers shortly after Bonnie and Clyde's death:

Now Bonnie and Clyde are the Barrow gang
I'm sure you all have read
how they rob and steal;
and those who squeal,
are usually found dying or dead.

They call them cold-blooded killers
they say they are heartless and mean.
But I say this with pride
that I once knew Clyde,
when he was honest and upright and clean.

But the law fooled around;
kept taking him down,
and locking him up in a cell.
Till he said to me;
'I'll never be free,
so I'll meet a few of them in hell.'

The road was so dimly lighted
there were no highway signs to guide.
But they made up their minds;
if all roads were blind,
they wouldn't give up till they died.

If they try to act like citizens
and rent them a nice little flat.
About the third night;
they're invited to fight,
by a sub-gun's rat-tat-tat.

They don't think they're too smart or desperate
they know that the law always wins.
They've been shot at before;
but they do not ignore,
that death is the wages of sin.

Some day they'll go down together
they'll bury them side by side.
To few it'll be grief,
to the law a relief
but it's death for Bonnie and Clyde.

THE PERFECT CRIME: LEOPOLD AND LOEB

Nathan Leopold and Richard Loeb were two Americans in their late teens living in Chicago. They both came from very wealthy families – each had an eye-popping monthly allowance of pocket money, and each grew up getting pretty much anything they ever wanted. They were also brilliant students – both were studying at university before they were fifteen and both intended to become lawyers!

Leopold spoke several languages fluently, and was such an expert on birds that he taught a class in ornithology and had a collection of over 3000 specimens. He was also a rather awkward and distant character. Loeb, on the other hand, was sporty, popular and handsome.

They became best friends in the early 1920s, partly because of the way their wealth, youth and unusual intelligence marked them out from their fellow students. These differences also led them to the twisted belief that they were better than those around them: they thought they could commit 'the perfect crime'.

Both Leopold and Loeb – 'Babe' and 'Dickie' as their families nicknamed them – had grown up breaking a few rules here and there, but the influence of their powerful families had always let them go unpunished.

They decided to commit a murder – one which would baffle the authorities and which no detective would ever solve.

They planned it for months. Once they'd picked a victim (someone of their own age, who came from an equally wealthy background), they would kidnap him. A ransom note would be sent to his parents. Meanwhile, the victim would be dead, his body hidden where nobody would ever find it. The parents would pay up. Leopold and Loeb would pocket the cash and never even be suspected. (They weren't doing it for the money, because they already had more money than they could ever need. They were doing it – and this is the real horror at the centre of their heartless crime – to prove what a superior pair they were, just for the hell of it.)

They considered several possible victims. One they rejected because he was too big and they'd have trouble lifting him. Another they rejected because they thought his father would be too mean to pay the ransom.

On Wednesday 21st May, 1924, they finally decided to simply pick the first person who happened to suit their purposes. The unlucky one was a distant cousin of Richard Loeb's, another teenager called Bobby Franks (whom Loeb had played tennis with only the day before). Leopold and Loeb had hired a car under a false name. They called Franks over and once he was in the car they beat him to death.

They drove out of town. So cold-hearted were they that they stopped for hot dogs, with Franks's body stashed in the back of the car. They hid Franks in a culvert (a drainage pipe beneath a railway line), posted a ransom note to Franks's parents, burnt the clothes they'd been wearing (to dispose of any forensic traces of the crime), cleaned out the rented car and then spent the evening playing cards.

Leopold and Loeb were confident they'd never be traced. Their ransom note arrived at the Franks's house the following day. However, the body was discovered at about the same time, by a man taking a short-cut close to the railway.

The case instantly hit the headlines. The police

investigation was headed by Robert Crowe, the local State's Attorney (a senior lawyer).

Detective Hugh Byrne of the Chicago police found a vital clue in the long grass close to the culvert: a pair of spectacles. The lenses turned out to be a very common prescription – there was little chance the owner could be traced through their optician – but further investigation showed that while the frames of the spectacles were also of a very common type, the hinges on them *were* unusual.

Painstaking record-checking by the police showed that there were only three people in the Chicago area who'd had hinges like that fitted to their glasses: one was a man who'd been abroad for a while, one was a lady who was wearing her glasses when the police called to see her, and the last was . . . Nathan Leopold.

Leopold claimed that he must have dropped them during one of his bird-watching trips. Ah, yes, now I remember, I stumbled while I was walking, and they must have fallen from my pocket.

Which pocket were they in, asked the police. The top pocket of this jacket, claimed Leopold.

The police asked him to put the spectacles in his pocket, and then demonstrate for them how he'd tripped. He did so, making a wide stumbling motion. The spectacles stayed tucked away in his pocket. The police had just proved that the tripping-over story was a lie.

The investigation turned up more solid evidence. Leopold and Loeb were part of a student study group that owned a typewriter that they took turns using. It was shown that the ransom note was typed using this machine.

The murderers had burnt their clothes and cleaned the hired car, but police managed to find plenty of bloodstains on the back seat of the vehicle once they tracked it down. Richard Loeb had used the name Mr Ballard when hiring the car and had checked into a nearby hotel using the same alias. At the hotel, investigators found a suitcase Loeb had left behind. And inside the case? A library book, checked out to 'R. A. Loeb'.

Far from committing 'the perfect crime', Leopold and Loeb had left a trail of clues! After they were arrested they began making up more stories to cover their tracks, which were very quickly proved false, and soon they were blaming each other for the whole idea. The two of them had one final thing in common: they were each sentenced to life in prison. Loeb was killed by another prisoner a few years later.

The Leopold-Loeb case, partly because of its 'Let's commit a crime just for the hell of it' aspect, has inspired loads of books (fiction and non-fiction), movies, magazine articles and TV dramas. Perhaps the most notable example is a very successful stage play called *Rope*, written in 1929 by a brillant writer named Patrick Hamilton (who had a very sad life story).

Hamilton denied that *Rope* was based on the case, saying he'd never heard of Leopold or Loeb. However, he was a great reader of true crime reports and it's almost impossible that he hadn't come across it. Although there are certainly differences between the play and the real-life case, there are too many similarities for it to be coincidence (as a detective might say!). *Rope* is a creepy piece of theatre and a very good example of how an actual investigation can influence fiction.

The Lindbergh Baby

Who's the most famous person on this planet, right now? A popstar, maybe? A politician? A reality TV star? In 1927, the fame of one man would have made today's superstars look like complete unknowns. And the kidnapping of that man's young son made headlines around the world.

Charles Lindbergh was an American inventor and engineer, a pioneer in the brand new field of aviation. In May 1927, at the age of 25, he became the first person to pilot an aeroplane, non-stop and alone, across the Atlantic Ocean. He took off from New York in his small aircraft called *Spirit of St Louis*, and once he'd landed at

Le Bourget Field near Paris, he instantly became the most celebrated and admired person on earth. There was barely anyone anywhere who didn't get to hear about 'Lucky Lindy', as they nicknamed him.

Hop forward five years to 1932. By then, Lindbergh was firmly established as the world's most glamorously heroic celebrity, and his wife and son – Charles Jnr – were equally famous.

On 1st March, the Lindberghs were staying at their country house near the town of Hopewell in New Jersey (not far from New York). At 8 pm, the live-in nanny put 20-month-old Charles Jnr to bed. At 9.30 pm, Lindbergh heard a bump and thought something had fallen over in the kitchen. At 10 pm, the nanny discovered that Charles Jnr had gone.

At first, she thought Lindbergh was playing one of his practical jokes. But he said he wasn't. Rushing to the nursery, they discovered a white envelope, perched on the sill of the open nursery window. It turned out to be a ransom note – one that was written in a weirdly misspelt and strangely worded way.

Police were on the scene half an hour later. News of what had happened spread like lightning. The son of Charles Lindbergh, Lucky Lindy, The Lone Eagle, had been kidnapped!

A foldaway, obviously homemade, ladder was

discovered in a bush near the house. There were footprints in the mud beneath the nursery window. The police made the kidnapping their top priority.

The following morning, the President of the United States, Herbert Hoover, declared that he would 'move heaven and earth' to get the child back safely. A reward of $75,000 was offered for information (equivalent to well over $1 million today). It wouldn't be an exaggeration to say that the media went bananas! They called it 'the crime of the century'.

And the result was: nothing. For days, the police were simply stumped.

A second ransom note arrived at the Lindberghs' house by post. This was also full of spelling mistakes and peculiar grammar. Because of the odd language used, it was thought that the kidnapper was foreign, possibly German. Lindbergh himself became convinced that gangsters were involved – although why is a mystery.

From that point on, the whole case became ever more complicated and confused. Lindbergh insisted on taking charge of the investigation himself, despite having no experience in law enforcement. Several well-meaning people put themselves forward to Lindbergh as helpers. One of them, a retired teacher called John Condon, managed to set up meetings with people who claimed to be in touch with the kidnappers. Others made similar claims, sometimes backed up with evidence and sometimes not, and on more than one occasion a huge sum of ransom money was handed over, only for it to vanish with no sign of Charles Jnr being returned.

On 12th May, several weeks after the kidnapping, a body was found, a few miles from the Lindberghs' home. Poor Charles Jnr appeared to have died the same night he'd been taken, and had never been held by the kidnappers at all.

Before ransom money had been handed over to 'the kidnappers' by John Condon, the police had made sure that every last banknote included in the package had a serial number that was part of a particular numerical sequence[1]. For thirty months, painstaking work by the New York Police Department and the FBI (see page 116)

---

[1] All banknotes have a multi-digit serial number printed on them. If you alert shops and businesses to be on the lookout for particular numbers, they can check the notes which are given to them and you can therefore work out where, when and by whom that money has been handled. (This is the reason you sometimes get stories and movies in which crooks demand 'non-sequential' banknotes – if they've got money with all kinds of random serial numbers on them, they're much harder for the police to track!)

tracked down any dollars from that ransom package that were spent. Eventually, the trail led them to a man called Bruno Hauptmann, a German immigrant.

Hauptmann had packages of the Lindbergh money hidden around his garage. A brilliant piece of forensic detective work by an expert on wood called Arthur Koehler put the lid on the investigation: Koehler took some of the wood from that home-made ladder, and not only matched up the lines and grooves of the wood with a section of floorboard missing from Hauptmann's attic, but even matched scratches on the wood to a tool in Hauptmann's toolkit.

You might think that this tragic episode had come to a conclusion, but nothing of the kind! The case continues to be debated and written about to this day – entire books have been devoted to examining the evidence. There are questions about many aspects of the case which have never been fully answered. For example:

1. Why were a number of very peculiar witnesses called at Hauptmann's trial? One man swore he saw Hauptmann on the day of the kidnapping, but his eyesight was so poor he couldn't possibly have identified anyone! John Condon claimed all the way through the investigation that he never clearly saw the kidnappers he had met, yet at the trial he

identified Hauptmann as one hundred per cent definitely the man he'd met.

2. Hauptmann absolutely insisted he was innocent, even after a newspaper offered him enough money to keep his wife and child in luxury for the rest of their lives, in exchange for a confession. Hauptmann had nothing more to lose by admitting what he'd done. Why keep on protesting he didn't do it?

3. If he was guilty, did Hauptmann act alone? If not, why were his accomplices never tracked down? If he hatched the whole plot himself, how could he possibly have known that the Lindberghs would be at their Hopewell house that night (they didn't normally live there, it was a last-minute change of plans), and how did he know which window to climb up to?

4. Hauptmann was a carpenter, who had ready access to wood and other materials. Why on earth would he make a ladder using a floorboard taken from his attic?

5. Charles Jnr had a couple of slightly deformed toes, and so did the body that was found. So why

was that body reckoned to be several centimetres taller than young Charles? Was it really him? If it wasn't, whatever happened to him?[2]

6. When the police examined the nursery, they found no fingerprints. Not one. Not Lindbergh's, not his wife's, not the nanny's, none whatsoever. How could any room be totally clean in that way? Had the nursery been wiped of evidence before the police showed up? If so, who did it?

The multiple mysteries surrounding the case of the Lindbergh baby inspired a number of works of fiction, both detective stories and others. The most famous was Agatha Christie's book, *Murder of the Orient Express*, featuring her Belgian detective Hercule Poirot, published in 1934.

In the book, the mystery is linked to an unsolved kidnapping from a family called Armstrong, rather than Lindbergh. Agatha Christie had travelled on the real Orient Express herself, and so could write about what it was like with authority. She was also inspired by a real-life

---

[2] Over the following decades, several people turned up claiming to BE the missing Lindburgh baby. Every one of them was a fake. Including the one who was female!

incident which had happened a few years earlier, when the same train had become stuck in a blizzard in Turkey and was unable to move for six days. In the book, the Orient Express gets trapped by a smiliar snowdrift (and there's a perfect example of Plot Device 4, as described on page 146).

THE FATAL FLAW

In detective fiction, you quite often come across the idea of a villain having some sort of 'fatal flaw' that gives them away: there's a lingering whiff of their distinctive perfume at the scene of the crime, for example, or their habit of constantly trimming their fingernails makes them drop incriminating clippings all over the place. That kind of obvious oddity isn't exactly common amongst real-life crooks, but the case of Willie Sutton is perhaps one of the few genuine examples. He was caught, for the final time, because of his clothes.

William Sutton – later nicknamed 'Slick Willie' and 'Willie the Actor' for reasons which will become clear in a minute – was born in New York in 1901. Like so many real-life crooks, he turned to crime at an early age, and had dropped out of school before he got to the equivalent of Year 8.

He tried a few legitimate jobs, including office clerk and gardener, but eighteen months was the longest time he ever held a normal job. He spent almost half his adult life locked up in prison for one crime or another.

Not that he was an unsuccessful villain: over a criminal career spanning forty years, it's estimated he stole over $2 million – equivalent to $32 million today – mostly from a grand total of over a hundred banks and jewellery shops. It's often said that he was perhaps the most polite bank robber around, always asking nicely for the bank cashiers to hand over the loot, while pointing a gun at them! 'You can't rob a bank on charm and personality,' he once said.

Although he was armed while committing every one of these hold-ups, he never fired his gun. He couldn't have anyway, since it was never loaded. Years later, when asked why not, he answered, 'Because someone might get hurt'!

You may already have guessed that Slick Willie was an unusual crook. He made several escape attempts from various prisons and managed to escape twice. Once, along with a dozen other prisoners, he got out through a tunnel they'd dug. On the other occasion, he used a gun which had been smuggled into the prison to force a guard to find him a ladder long enough to scale the prison's nine-metre walls! He dressed up in the guard's uniform, and when searchlights from the prison's watchtowers picked him out halfway up the ladder, he simply turned and waved, and shouted, 'It's OK!'. The guards were fooled long enough for him to get to freedom!

His prison guard disguise demonstrates the reason for his nicknames. He was very skilled at pretending to be post office workers, cops, messengers or maintenance men. He would walk into banks or shops, often first thing in the morning when they were just opening up, and the staff wouldn't suspect a thing until they had a pistol aimed at them.

Willie Sutton's expertise at disguise grew out of his lifelong habit of stylish dressing. While not robbing banks, he was someone who demanded only the very best and most fashionable attire. He was extremely fussy about his appearance – and here's where the 'fatal flaw' idea comes in.

In 1950, Sutton was added to the FBI's list of *Most Wanted* crooks and it was decided to use his own fussiness as a weapon against him! His picture and description were circulated to all the expensive clothes shops and tailors in the areas where he was known to have committed crimes.

The tactic paid off in 1952. A twenty-four-year-old tailor from New York, who fancied himself as a bit of an amateur detective, recognised Slick Willie while on the New York subway. He followed Sutton to a garage, then immediately reported what he'd found to the police.

At his trial, Willie Sutton was sentenced to a further thirty years in jail, on top of the life sentence 'plus one hundred and five years' he'd been serving when he escaped. He was let out at the end of 1969 on health grounds, suffering from emphysema (a lung disease).

Believe it or not, Slick Willie was by then such a well-known name that shortly after his release he appeared in a TV commercial for a bank's new photo-ID credit card! 'They call it the face card,' he said to the camera. 'Now when I say I'm Willie Sutton, people believe me.'

THE
WATERGATE SCANDAL

Detective stories often feature detectives who aren't actual police officers or private eyes – Agatha Christie's Miss Marple, for example, or Margery Allingham's Albert Campion . . . or your very own Saxby Smart! You rarely find that sort of thing happening in real life, but one notable exception is the Watergate Scandal which outraged America in the 1970s.

It began on the night of 17th June 1972. A security guard at the Watergate office building in Washington DC noticed that the latches on several doors had been taped over (so that they wouldn't lock). Mystified, he removed the tape. An hour later, when his patrolling led him back through the same corridors, he saw that the same doors had been re-taped! He called the police. Five burglars were arrested.

The men had been stealing papers and placing secret wire taps (phone bugs) in the offices of the Democratic National Committee, which was part of the Democratic Party, one of the two main political parties in America.

Here's where our non-police detectives come in. When the burglary was made public, it interested two reporters who worked for *The Washington Post* newspaper, Bob Woodward and Carl Bernstein. It seemed strange that these burglars had apparently come all the way from Miami, hundreds of miles away, to break into these offices. It seemed even more strange that they were found to be carrying thousands of dollars in cash with them.

Woodward and Bernstein began to write a series of articles for the *Post* in which they uncovered more and more information about the break-in, about the official investigation that had followed it, and about the people who had been involved. It turned out that all five of the burglars had been paid large sums of money linked to the Committee to Re-Elect the President (or CREEP, as it was rather unfortunately known!). One of the burglars was even on the staff of CREEP.

This committee was an organisation which was

campaigning on behalf of the US Republican President, Richard Nixon. A presidential election was due to take place later in the year.

It was also discovered that an ex-CIA agent and an ex-FBI agent had been in a hotel room opposite the Watergate offices, using walkie-talkies to direct the burglars where to go. These agents were now working for the White House, the American equivalent of 10 Downing Street!

Despite the strange and suspicious circumstances which surrounded the Watergate break-in, it still wasn't headline news outside Washington. Even Woodward and Bernstein's fellow journalists thought that they were getting tangled up in a knot of false accusations. Richard Nixon was a popular president, and he easily won the election.

But Woodward and Bernstein wouldn't give up. Without their investigations, it's possible that the full story may never have been uncovered.

And it was a jaw-dropper of a story! What had started as a suspicious burglary gradually snowballed into an enormous political scandal. High-up officials in the White House, and in the Republican Party, had got up to all kinds of dirty tricks – almost all illegal – to spy on the Democratic Party and try to undermine their chances in the election. Official enquiries were launched. One by one, people connected to the conspiracy were found out and put in prison. For two years or more, Richard Nixon himself denied all knowledge of what had been going on – he famously said that 'there can be no whitewash at the White House'.

He was lying. As more and more of his advisors turned out to be involved in the plot, Nixon found himself cornered. The most damning evidence against him was a series of secret recordings he'd made of his meetings with various officials. One of them – known as the 'Smoking Gun' tape – clearly showed that he'd known the truth all along.

President Nixon resigned in disgrace in August 1974. He was the first and only US president to leave office in this way.

A Portrait of Infamous Art Thefts

When it comes to stealing a famous work of art, there's one giant-sized, elephant-in-the-room problem – what are you going to do with it once you've got it?

Stolen money can be easily exchanged and most stolen items can be sold, but what can you do with a unique piece of artwork? Either keep it hidden and hope the cops don't notice, or sell it to someone equally crooked who's prepared to pay you for something they'll have to keep hidden. On the face of it, stealing art doesn't make sense, and yet it happens regularly.

A Few Cases from the Files

1. In 1994, *The Scream* by Edvard Munch (that one with a bald person holding their head beside a railing) was stolen by four men who left a note behind which said, *Thanks for the poor security*. It was recovered three months later. *The Scream* was stolen again in 2004!

2. Thieves raided the Museum of Art in Sao Paolo, Brazil, in 2007. They got away with around £38 million's worth of paintings. When they were recovered, the paintings were escorted back to the museum by a hundred police officers.

3. Two men wearing false moustaches and police uniforms walked into the Isabella Stewart Gardner Museum in Boston, USA, in March 1990. They walked out with around £200 million's worth of pictures by artists such as Manet, Rembrandt and Degas. Not one of them has ever been found.

4. More than twenty paintings and sculptures were taken from a private collection in Madrid in 2001. The gangsters who'd agreed to buy the stuff from the thieves wanted it all to be authenticated before they'd pay: enter a team of undercover cops posing as art experts!

Stealing a Masterpiece

The *Mona Lisa* by Leonardo da Vinci is perhaps the most famous painting in the world. It was also the subject of perhaps the most notorious art theft of all time.

In 1911, the Louvre museum in Paris placed glass panels in front of a number of its exhibits to keep them safe from vandalism. The glass used was very reflective and a lot of people protested about it. One of them was an artist called Louis Beraud, and on August 22nd he decided to take direct action. He would walk into the Louvre, go up to the *Mona Lisa*, and paint a picture on the glass of a young lady doing her hair. This would be his way of saying: Get rid of that glass.

Into the Louvre he stomped. He marched to the room where the *Mona Lisa* was hung, and . . . no *Mona Lisa*. No glass either. Beraud asked a security guard what was going on. The guard didn't know. Maybe the painting was away being photographed? Nobody seemed to know where it was. In fact, it took until the next day for it to be established that the *Mona Lisa* had indeed been stolen!

The Louvre was closed for the next week, to allow a team of sixty investigators to work undisturbed. All they found was the *Mona Lisa*'s wooden frame (and that pesky sheet of glass) on a staircase.

It was reckoned that the theft had occurred early the previous morning, at a time when only museum staff had access to it. Despite extensive questioning and investigation of over eight hundred suspects, no member of staff was found who might have done it.

The whole of France was up in arms. Many theories were discussed in the newspapers. Ships and trains leaving the country were searched top to bottom. People even lined up to see the empty space where the painting had been!

Several dodgy art dealers and known art thieves were investigated, but without success. Even the famous artist Pablo Picasso was suspected for a while. The trail soon went cold and the theft of the *Mona Lisa* looked like it would remain a mystery forever.

Two years later, out of the blue, an art dealer in Florence, Italy, was contacted by someone who called himself 'Leonardo'. This Leonardo asked for his help in selling the *Mona Lisa*. The dealer, whose name was Alfredo Geri, assumed 'Leonardo' must have a good copy – not the real thing.

Geri agreed to meet the man, whose real name was Vincenzo Peruggia, at a hotel in Milan. Geri went to the meeting with Giovanni Poggi, director of the Uffizi Museum in Florence. Peruggia produced a large trunk. Inside, hidden in a secret compartment underneath a load of underwear and shirts, was the *Mona Lisa*. The real one!

Geri and Poggi could hardly believe their eyes. Vincenzo Peruggia was immediately handed over to the police.

It turned out that, until this meeting, the painting had never left Paris. Peruggia had worked at the Louvre a few years earlier, so he knew exactly when and how to accomplish the theft. He'd even helped make that glass screen it was placed behind!

Today, the *Mona Lisa* is still behind glass in the Louvre in Paris – non-reflective, bullet-proof glass this time. Someone sprayed red paint at it in 1974, and in 2009 the glass was cracked when a Russian woman hurled a souvenir from the museum's gift shop at it. But, so far, the lady in the painting continues to smile down at the tourists.

ROBBERY!
A HANDFUL OF
INFAMOUS HEISTS

The Antwerp Diamond Heist

The biggest diamond robbery in history took place in Antwerp in Belgium in 2003. Around £200 million's worth of diamonds were stolen from the Antwerp Diamond Centre – so many that the thieves couldn't carry them all and dropped a few on the way out. It wasn't only the size of the theft which amazed police: the diamonds were stolen from what was supposed to be the most secure vault in the entire world!

The vault was protected by ten layers of security, including infrared heat detectors, cameras, a magnetic field, movement sensors, twenty-four-hour guards and a thirty-centimetre thick steel door with a lock that had a hundred million possible combinations.

The theft was planned for more than two years, with one of the gang even renting space in the office building above the vault, posing as an Italian diamond trader (there are many such traders in Antwerp). On the night of the raid, 15th February, fake tapes were inserted into the security system and cameras were covered up. Light sensors were blocked with tape and the motion and heat detectors were disabled using hairspray. The vault was two floors underground and contained 189 private safety deposit boxes. Over a hundred of the boxes were opened using a specially-made device like a giant corkscrew.

Despite the ingenious nature of the theft, the gang – four men in all – were caught simply because one of them failed to burn a bag of evidence. The diamonds themselves have never been recovered.

The Perfect Crime . . . Nearly

At 7.30 pm on 17th January 1950, five heavily disguised robbers turned up at the offices of a security firm in Boston, USA. They wore gloves to avoid leaving fingerprints, and thickly-soled sneakers to avoid making a noise. Some employees of the firm, who were just closing up the company safe on the second floor for the day, were forced to hand over $1.2 million in cash and another $1.5 million in bank securities. It was the biggest robbery in American history up to that time.

The police were left clueless. The crooks hadn't left a trace behind and the identity of the thieves was a complete mystery. The raid was called 'the perfect crime' . . . until the crooks gave themselves away.

There'd been eleven of them in all. They'd agreed that after the money was split between them, they would all lie low, do nothing suspicious and wait – maybe even for a couple of years – until the cops closed the case and went away scratching their heads.

But most of the gang were habitual thieves who had great difficulty keeping out of trouble! Several were arrested for other crimes and they started to bicker among themselves about who got what. One of them, Joseph O'Keefe, made more of a noise than the others. After several attempts on his life to silence him, O'Keefe confessed all to the police and the gang was rounded up.

The Krupp Diamond

The Krupp Diamond is a very large and famous jewel, about the size of a marble. In 1959, it sat at the centre of a ring owned by Vera Krupp, the American ex-wife of a wealthy German industrialist. One evening in April, at her large ranch near Las Vegas, three men broke in, tied her up, tore the ring from her finger (almost breaking it in the process) and took $700,000 in cash. She managed to raise the alarm, and FBI agents quickly realised that this was probably the work of a man called John Hagenson.

By brilliant detective work? No, because Hagenson had been stupid enough to try a very similar robbery a few weeks earlier, in California (although, of course, not stealing anything as valuable as the Krupp diamond).

Hagenson was tracked halfway across America, from Nevada to Louisiana, where he was arrested. His arrest set the FBI on the trail of the others, and the diamond was found near New York, in the lining of a coat belonging to one of the thieves.

The diamond was replaced in the ring, which was later bought by the actor Richard Burton as a present for the actress Elizabeth Taylor.

The Brinks Mat Robbery

The biggest gold heist in British history took place in November 1983, when six robbers broke into the Brinks Mat warehouse at Heathrow Airport early one morning. They'd expected to find around £3 million in cash. What they actually found when they opened the safe was 6,800 gold bars, valued at about $26 million.

Several members of the gang had to go and find extra

vehicles to transport all the extra gold, and they used the warehouse's forklift truck to move it. They finally drove away a few minutes before security guards arrived to take over the day shift from the guards the gang had violently attacked and tied up.

The thieves began to use their gangland connections to have the gold melted down and sold on. Meanwhile, Commander Frank Cater of Scotland Yard's Flying Squad was put in charge of the investigation. The police came to the conclusion that the way the robbery had been carried out pointed to an inside job. Sure enough, one of the security guards turned out to be living with the sister of Brian Robinson, a gangster known as 'The Colonel'. Robinson, and an armed robber called Michael McAvoy, were already top of the police's list of suspects.

Robinson and McAvoy didn't exactly make things difficult for Cater's team: they hadn't assembled their gang with much secrecy. What's more, within weeks of the robbery, the pair of them moved from humble South London council homes to large estates in Kent, which they paid for with cash. It's also been rumoured that two Rottweiler dogs were bought to guard the new mansions, and were named . . . Brinks and Mat.

Although the ringleaders were rounded up, none of the gold was ever recovered. The haul was so huge, it's been claimed that anyone who's bought gold jewellery in the UK since the mid-1980s may well be wearing a tiny piece of the Brinks Mat bullion!

The Great Train Robbery

For 125 years, a nightly Post Office train known as the 'Up Special' ran from Glasgow to London carrying postal deliveries and cash. At just past 3 am on 8th August 1963, the train stopped for what turned out to be a bogus red signal.

Fifteen masked men boarded the train. One of the gang badly injured the train's driver. They separated the engine and the first two carriages from the rest of the train – which was full of postal workers sorting mail – and drove on a mile ahead. Then the thieves bundled one hundred and twenty mail and money bags into a van and drove off. They'd stolen £2.6 million (equivalent to around £40 million today). The postal workers remained unaware of the robbery until it was all over.

The police launched a massive hunt for the men and the van they'd used. Five days after the robbery, the gang's hideout was identified as Leatherslade Farm, about twenty miles from the scene of the crime. As the police closed in, the robbers fled, and in doing so they sealed their fate: they'd left their fingerprints all over the house!

In took several years to finally round up and jail the

whole gang. A couple of them managed to escape abroad, but eventually gave themselves up; a couple more escaped from prison and went on the run. To this day, the Great Train Robbery is one of the most notorious crimes in modern British history.

EXHIBIT B:
YOU'RE NICKED!

THE WORLD OF
REAL-LIFE DETECTIVES

REAL-LIFE POLICING AND REAL-LIFE crimes which have always been the inspiration for detective stories. They say that real life is stranger than fiction and that's certainly true when it comes to law enforcement. Some of the stuff here simply wouldn't be believed in a story and some of it shows that the life of a real detective is nothing like the life of a fictional one. But it's all true!

Saxby

PART 1:

HERE COME THE COPS!

(NOTES ON THE REAL WORK OF POLICE OFFICERS)

IN THE YEARS BC (BEFORE COPS)

For hundreds of years, the only form of law enforcement in Britain was based around feudal ideas brought over by the Saxons (feudalism was the Medieval system of government, in which ordinary folk were controlled by local leaders who in turn served the King). People were divided into groups, and those groups reported to a county sheriff who was responsible for maintaining order.

After 1361, a network of local Justices of the Peace was set up. These JPs were helped by a parish constable – the official person in each town or village who was supposed to uphold the law. However, these constables were mostly pretty useless, partly because it was a job all able-bodied men took their turn in doing, but mostly because it was part-time work that was virtually unpaid. Most constables were open to bribery, and few were keen on their duties. The constables' assistants, the night-watchmen, nicknamed charleys, were even worse: they were usually older men who'd fallen on hard times and the majority of them were nowhere to be seen after dark!

Then 'thief-takers', prominent in the 1700s, started to appear after an Act of Parliament in 1697 offered rewards for the capture of criminals (see the section on Jonathan Wild on page 21). The thief-takers were bounty hunters rather than law-enforcers: they were only in it for the money, and took little interest in whether the person they caught was guilty or not. The reward for capturing a highwayman, coiner or burglar was about £40, the equivalent of several years' wages for most people. The whole system of thief-taking was corrupt from start to finish, and was deeply unpopular with almost everyone, on both sides of the law.

The need for an organised approach to crime in towns and cities became urgent. It was taken for granted that nobody with any sense ever left their home after sunset. The famous writer Dr Samuel Johnson, in his 1738 poem *London*, said:

Prepare for death, if here at night you roam
And sign your will before you sup from home.

In 1749, the novelist Henry Fielding was given the job of magistrate (a type of judge) at the Bow Street Magistrates' Court in London. Disgusted at the lawless state of the capital's streets, he set up a group of constables who became known as the Bow Street Runners.

Including Fielding himself, there were only eight of them in London. They were mostly roughneck locals who had a good knowledge of London's underworld, but among them was Fielding's blind brother John. He took over from Henry in 1754 and became known as 'the blind beak of Bow Street' – it was said he could recognise the voices of three thousand crooks, and could tell if any of them were lying just by listening to them.

The Bow Street Runners didn't patrol London as such – they brought people to court on the say-so of the magistrates. Sometimes they travelled right across the country in search of particular villains. After a few years, the Runners established a team on horseback, who became known as Robin Redbreasts because of their uniforms. There was even a Bow Street Runners magazine called the *Covent Garden Journal*, which gave the public information about crimes and criminals, not unlike a number of TV shows do today!

Look Out, It's the Peelers!

The arrival of Robert Peel as Home Secretary in 1822 marked the beginning of a *huge* change in the way crime was dealt with in Britain. Until the 1820s, all efforts were concentrated on punishment. There were over four hundred crimes that carried the death penalty, including pick-pocketing more than a shilling (5p) or stealing anything worth more than £2.

Peel replaced these punishments with ones which were more in keeping with the nature of the crimes. Efforts were now to be concentrated on *preventing* crime rather than simply punishing it.

The Metropolitan Police Act of 1829 set up the world's

very first police force, to cover the London area. The first police officers went out on patrol on the evening of Friday 25th September 1829 and policemen (they were all men in those days) soon became known as 'peelers' or 'bobbies' after their founder.

Scotland Where-Was-It?

It's not known for sure why the first Metropolitan Police Headquarters in London was ever called Scotland Yard, because it was in Whitehall Place. There was never a yard there and it certainly wasn't in Scotland. The HQ moved in 1890 to Victoria Embankment, but was called New Scotland Yard. Even more confusingly, when it moved again in 1967 to Broadway in south-west London, the name New Scotland Yard was kept.

Things didn't go smoothly for the peelers at first. It was very difficult to recruit reliable officers: of the first 2,800 men hired, only about 600 kept their jobs. Far too many joined up because they were unfit for other work, or because they liked the idea of being able to boss people about legally! The very first policeman hired was sacked after only a couple of hours. He was drunk.

For some time, the peelers were very unpopular with the public. A lot of people worried that having an official police force would lead to ordinary people being spied on, or arrested if they didn't support the government, in exactly the same way as people today worry about civil liberties (freedom from official interference or surveillance, e.g. CCTV cameras).

A lot of effort was put into reassuring people that the police were there to help them. Peelers were deliberately given blue uniforms rather than more visible red ones because the army had red uniforms at the time and most people associated the army with trouble. The first peelers wore tall hats reinforced with cane, partly so that

The Old Bill

The police have long been nicknamed The Bill or The Old Bill. There are many theories as to why:

1. 'Old Bill' was Victorian slang for a bribe offered to a policeman.

2. The name comes from the bills, or billhooks, that some early police carried as weapons.

3. It refers to the legal Bills which pass through parliament to create laws.

they could be seen in a crowd, and partly so that they could stand on their hats to look over walls. The large buttons on their uniforms were supposed to remind people of the sort of outfits that servants wore, to add to the impression that the police were helpers and not a military force.

The life of a peeler was far from easy. The wages were low and most peelers had to do seven shifts a week – day and night – patrolling for miles, in all weathers, and they were forbidden to stop for a sit-down!

Police forces started to be set up across the rest of Britain from 1833 onwards. A gradual reduction in overall rates of crime was what eventually persuaded the public that having a police force was a good idea.

What Does a Modern Police Detective Do, Exactly?

CID detectives – Criminal Investigation Department detectives – work in plain clothes. Uniformed police officers can apply to become CID detectives. After passing an exam and doing a four-week course, they're then tutored by an experienced detective before being allowed to work on their own. They simply add the word 'Detective' to their rank – so, a Police Constable would become a Detective Constable (DC), a Sergeant would become a Detective Sergeant (DS) and so on.

All reported crimes are allocated to a DC, who becomes that case's Officer in The Case (OIC – yes, there are *lots* of abbreviations used in everyday police work).

Most small-scale, everyday crimes will be handled by that one DC, overseen by a DS.

A case which requires more investigation may involve the next rank up, a Detective Inspector (DI), who will direct the investigation. Detective Chief Inspectors (DCIs) only get involved in very serious crimes. Most DCs will be handling a number of different cases, at different stages of investigation, at any one time.

At every stage of a case, detailed records are kept of exactly who did what and when. There is a written account of every decision made in the case by the officer(s) in charge. A great deal of what the police do is governed by PACE, the Police And Criminal Evidence Act, which sets out how police work should be carried out.

Case Breakdown

Most criminal investigations can be broken down into three main areas:

The Evidence Bit – This is the 'whodunit' part of the case. There are three sorts of evidence:

1. Evidence from WITNESSES. Eye-witnesses are people who saw the crime taking place. Other witnesses include anyone who might know something relevant to

the case. A witness's evidence is recorded as a written 'statement'.

2. PHYSICAL evidence. Clothing, weapons, DNA samples, vehicles, anything gathered at the scene of the crime . . . the possibilities are endless. Detectives don't do forensic tests themselves – that's a different job entirely. Evidence is always labelled, and it's signed for, timed and dated every single time it's handled by anyone.

3. Evidence from CCTV. With so many cameras pointed in so many directions in most towns and cities, it's often possible to track the movements of cars or people involved in a crime. This can involve going through many, many hours of recordings, and is extremely painstaking (and boring!) work.

Bank Robbery

Technically, a bank itself isn't 'robbed'. Breaking into a building and taking stuff is burglary. Robbery is theft where force or threats are used against someone. For theft from a bank to be called a 'bank robbery', a person must have been hurt or threatened.

The Dealing with Suspects Bit – Arrested suspects are taken to a 'custody unit' at a police station, and their details are logged on a computer system. Normally, they are only allowed in their cell, or in an interview room. Interviews with suspects are recorded and suspects are usually accompanied by a solicitor (a lawyer who can advise them). The police have a duty of 'disclosure' to the solicitor, meaning that they must give the solicitor enough information about how and why the suspect has been arrested so that the solicitor can properly advise their client. In serious cases, questions police officers ask suspects are carefully prepared before the interview and will often be compiled by specialists, to make sure that the suspect is asked enough questions about every aspect of the case.

The Legal Bit – This is the part you often don't encounter in detective stories or dramas! During anything more than routine investigations, the police will regularly consult with the CPS (the Crown Prosecution Service, the organisation which takes cases to court). They check what evidence they need to gather in order for the suspect to be found guilty in court. For serious crimes, detectives will talk to the CPS before even arresting a suspect. There's a great deal of time and fiddly paperwork involved in bringing a case to court.

OK, So the Bank's Been Burgled . . .

The bank's alarm is ringing! Someone call the cops!

1. Uniformed officers will always be first at the scene. They will do preliminary work such as cordoning off the area (putting up that black and yellow tape) and identifying any eye-witnesses.

2. Detectives will arrive about half an hour later. For a major incident, a DI will take charge. A 'policy book' is started, in which notes are taken about everything that happens, as it happens.

3. Major investigations are based around specific 'Actions'. These are particular tasks which are allocated to particular officers or groups of officers. The total number of staff involved varies depending on the crime.

4. The total number of staff involved in the investigation will vary enormously (it all depends on what's happened!), but back at HQ the overall team will include:

– Senior Investigating Officer (SIO)
– Deputy SIO
– An OIC (Officer In the Case, who's always a DC)
– Disclosure officer (responsible for providing

info to suspects and their solicitor)
– Office manager (to organise everyday stuff –
  sometimes a DC, sometimes a civilian)
– Various teams who carry out Actions
– Interview team(s) – usually DCs
– Statement review team (who check through
  written evidence to make sure it makes sense
  and answer all the questions that need asking)
– Scene Of Crime Officers (SOCO, sometimes
  called CSI, Crime Scene Investigators – usually
  civilians rather than police officers)
– Search teams (if needed – uniformed officers
  who search the crime scene and other areas for
  evidence)
– Intelligence cell (who track down other
  information relating to the case).

A Quick Note About Computers

Mobile phones, netbooks and desktop computers can provide vital evidence. However, examining them is a much more technical task than you might think – just switching a computer on can alter information on it, which will affect how it can be used as evidence! Gathering evidence from gadgets can take experts a LONG time.

That Wouldn't Happen!

Some ways in which TV and movies get detective work wrong:

1. Senior officers like DIs and DCIs *never* get involved in interviewing witnesses, examining crime scenes and so on. DCs do that.

2. DCs are *never* the first ones at a crime scene. Uniformed officers are.

3. The same officer would *never* attend a crime scene then do an interview or arrest a suspect relating to the same case. There'd be a risk of 'cross contamination' of evidence (fibres from a crime scene accidentally getting on to an innocent suspect, for example).

4. Most crime dramas take place over a couple of days. Real cases *never* (well, hardly ever) get solved that fast.

5. Lights and sirens are *never* used when going to arrest anyone (it'd warn them the cops were coming!), and almost *never* used when taking a suspect away. They are for emergency response *only*.

6. Real officers *never* call each other by their ranks. A DC or PC might call a sergeant 'Sarge', or a senior officer 'sir' or 'ma'am', but nobody ever addresses anyone else as 'DC Smith' or 'DCI Jones' (or even 'Constable') – they just call each by their names! Even junior officers will call senior officers 'John' or 'Jane'.

7. Mobile phones are *never* trackable to within a metre or two. Tracking a phone is very complicated and *never* accomplished as easily as on TV.

8. CCTV footage can *never* be 'cleaned up'. It can be improved slightly, but you can't use computers or anything else to 'extract' or clarify images.

9. You would *never* see a uniformed PC standing guard in an interview room. Crime dramas are full of interviews in which suspects are interrogated with a cop standing by the door. This doesn't happen. Ever.

THE FBI: AMERICA'S SCOTLAND YARD

The FBI, or Federal Bureau of Investigation, is an American organisation you'll often hear mentioned in movies or cop shows. It investigates over 200 types of crimes, as well as issues of national security (making it partly like Scotland Yard, and partly like MI5).

In America, at the beginning of the twentieth century, crooks were becoming increasingly mobile, as cars became more common and better roads were built. People were free to cross the borders between the different individual states that make up the United States but law enforcement officers only had power in their own states. Crooks took advantage of this by crossing into different states so they couldn't be caught (see Bonnie and Clyde on page 55).

America needed a 'federal' law enforcement service – one which could deal with crimes which crossed these state boundaries or involved more than one state. The first moves towards creating such a service came in 1908 but this Bureau of Investigation only really began to be effective after 1924 when J. Edgar Hoover (a controversial figure in American history) took over as director. Crime-related information, such as fingerprint records, started to be centralised in the Bureau of Investigation's files. A number of high-profile cases, such as the Lindbergh kidnapping (see page 68) and the Prohibition-era gangsters caused changes in the law which made inter-state investigations much easier.

In 1932, the first issue of what would become the *FBI Law Enforcement Bulletin* was published (this was where the term Public Enemy Number One was coined – see page 41). The public was impressed by what the Bureau was doing, and it wasn't long before being one of their agents was a much sought-after job. In 1935, it became known as the Federal Bureau of Information.

Sting 1 and Sting 2

Here's a true story from the files of the FBI. In the autumn of 1975, a rather dingy office supplies business called PFF Inc. opened up a warehouse in Washington DC. Word soon got around that PFF was a 'front' (an apparently legitimate business masking criminal activity) for a bunch of New York gangsters.

Stolen goods began to be traded at the warehouse. Thieves turned up and would be paid a small sum of money in return for PFF taking the goods off their hands. Over $1 million's worth of stuff was brought in: TVs, cars, trucks, motorcycles, electronics, guns, you name it. They took in a lot of stolen office supplies, and even a bearskin.

PFF sent out party invitations to all its 'customers' the following February. It wanted to, er, 'celebrate' the success of the, ahem, 'business', ha ha. About sixty crooks turned up for the event.

Every last one of them was led away in handcuffs. PFF was indeed a front . . . for the FBI. All the PFF staff were undercover agents. They had gathered plenty of evidence against the crooks and had now rounded up an impressive number of them in one evening.

PFF had stood for Police-FBI Front.

The operation, which had been run jointly by the FBI and the Washington Metropolitan Police Department, was known as Sting 1 and was such a success that they decided to try it all over again.

Five months later, a whole new collection of crooks

was arrested after they came to a garage owned by a company called GYA, clutching what they thought were winning lottery tickets. GYA? Got Ya Again. Sting 1 had been featured in the news quite prominently and yet Sting 2 got even better results!

By the end of the whole operation, the FBI had arrested over three hundred criminals and recovered over $3.4 million in stolen property.

PART 2:

THREE CHEERS FOR TECHNOLOGY!

(NOTES ON FORENSICS, THE SCIENCE OF DETECTIVE WORK)

BALLISTICS

Ballistics, in detective work, is the study of guns and the different forms of damage they do. Every investigation of this kind has to consider five elements of each shot fired:

1. The firearm/weapon used
2. The bullet
3. The cartridge-case
4. The trajectory of the bullet (the path followed by the bullet from gun to target)
5. The bullet's point of impact.

The first three of these elements need to be matched

up together. This relies partly on a detailed knowledge of gun manufacturers and models, and partly on a microscope. The inside of a gun's barrel leaves tiny marks on the bullets it fires, in a way that is different for every individual gun. You can tell which gun fired which bullet by comparing the marks left on the bullets.

A famous case of ballistics in action is the case of PC Gutteridge, who was shot dead in Essex in 1927. He was found by a roadside, and had died so swiftly that he had fallen back on to the grass with his pencil and policeman's notepad still held in his hands. Vital ballistic evidence came in the form of a spent gun cartridge, which had a distinctive scar along one side where the part of the gun which fired it was damaged. The revolver was found after a search of one of the suspects' homes, and it was matched to the scarred cartridge. This case helped establish ballistics as a regular part of police work.

The trajectory of the bullet is important because it shows a detective where a bullet was fired from. Suppose you find a bullet embedded into a wall – the angle of the miniature 'tunnel' it made as it went in can be used to establish the line along which the bullet travelled (by simple geometry – you extend the straight line of the 'tunnel' backwards). Following that line back will give you a very good idea of the exact position of the gun when the bullet was fired.

The impact point of a bullet can reveal a lot about how close the gun was fired, what angle it was fired at, and so on. Bullets often don't 'fly' straight – they spin, wobble as they move through the air, and can even tumble head over heels – and these variations are shown in different impact point patterns.

Leaving Its Mark

It's possible to test a suspect's clothes and skin to discover if they've recently fired a gun, thanks to gunshot residue. Whenever a gun is fired, microscopic particles from the bullet, the cartridge it was in, and even the gun itself are blasted into the air (hardly surprising since every shot is basically a small explosion!). These particles, which are far too small to see and which don't get washed away, can be found using chemical tests or electron microscopes.

BLOOD

Blood is very useful stuff, and not only when it's inside our bodies! It can also be of great help to the detective, in several ways.

Blood Tests

Until the twentieth century, it wasn't even possible to confirm that a suspected bloodstain was really blood at all! Developed in 1901, the Preciptin Test could distinguish human blood from animal blood. Over the following decades, various chemical methods were devised which could extract more and more detailed information from blood samples, both fresh and dried up. Although a number of these tests have since been replaced by DNA profiling (see below), simple blood tests are still useful to determine if, for example, a person is taking medicines or has been drinking alcohol or taking drugs.

Droplet Patterns

A surprising amount of information can be got from observing spots of liquid on different surfaces – not just blood, this applies to most thicker-than-water liquids.

1. Height

A droplet that has fallen straight down, from a height of about half a metre or less, will normally appear as a simple, rounded blob. The greater the distance the droplet falls, the rougher the edges of the blob appear and the more mini-droplets are thrown out as it hits the surface. By closely examining how far a droplet has 'splattered', you can get a good estimate of how far the droplet fell in the first place.

2. Movement

It's easy to tell whether a droplet fell from something or someone who was moving at the time. Droplets falling from something that is *stationary* look like the rounded blobs described above. Droplets falling from something that is *moving* have a shape rather like an exclamation mark, with an elongated part with a smaller 'dot' at one end.

3. Direction

In cases where you have an 'exclamation mark' droplet pattern, you can tell which direction the movement was in by looking at the smaller dot – the dot will appear on the end facing the direction the person was headed.

4. Angle

Exclamation mark patterns can also tell you at what angle the droplets hit the surface they're on – the longer the exclamation mark, the smaller the angle of impact. This is useful for estimating how fast the droplet was going, and how close to impact it was when it began to fall.

Observing smear patterns in liquids can be useful too. If you find droplets which have been brushed against, or spread out on a surface, this helps you put together a picture of what physical actions have taken place. The direction in which the liquid is smeared is also an indicator of the direction of movement.

DNA

The most important way in which blood can help a detective is in the DNA it contains. DNA is Deoxyribonucleic Acid, the basic chemical structure out of which all living things on the planet are built. It's found in *any* biological traces of a person, not just blood – hair, skin cells, nails, anything. We shed stuff and leave everything from saliva to skin oil all over the place, all the time (yucky, but true). A person's DNA profile is every bit as unique as their fingerprints and it can be extracted from even a tiny physical trace left at a crime scene.

The Science Bit

Exactly *how* our genes are constructed of DNA, and *how* a DNA sample gives us unique personal information, is a mind-bogglingly complex subject. 99.9% of genetic material is identical in all humans, and there are various types of analysis used to pick out the tiny minority of DNA sequences which are useful for detectives. Ask your science teacher about it!

DNA profiling, or genetic fingerprinting as it's sometimes called, was developed in the 1980s by Sir Alec Jeffreys at the University of Leicester. The first time it was used during a criminal investigation was in 1986.

Police suspected that a young man called Robert Buckland had been involved in a murder at the village of Enderby (oddly not far from Jeffreys's lab at Leicester). They already knew that this murder was linked to another case from three years earlier.

Jeffreys conducted DNA tests on samples from both the crime scenes and on Buckland's blood. The results were 100% definite: the same man *had* committed both crimes. However, that man *wasn't* Robert Buckland. The real killer was also identified using DNA analysis. Ever since this clear-cut example, genetic fingerprinting has become a routine part of serious crime investigations all over the world.

FINGERPRINTS

Everyone, even identical twins, has their own unique set of fingerprints. This fact has been massively useful to detectives for well over a hundred years. Every police agency on earth uses fingerprinting.

For centuries, the ancient Chinese used thumbprints to seal documents, and the seventeenth century anatomist, Marcello Malpighi, went to great pains to describe fingertip ridges. However, it wasn't until 1880 that fingerprints were suggested as a way of identifying people. In 1892, the English scientist Sir Francis Galton worked out a method for classifying prints, using three of the features you see on them: arches, loops and whorls (spirally shapes).

Later Sir Edward Henry, head of the CID, included tented arches and divided loops into two sorts, and so there were five features. The Henry system was rapidly adopted all over the world and modern fingerprint ID systems are still based on it today (with a few additions and refinements!).

The Acid Test

It is a myth that fingerprints can be 'burnt off' your fingers using acid – they grow back! John Dillinger tried that (see page 43) and it didn't work. Another crook, called Robert Phillips, had skin grafts from his chest put over his prints! That didn't work either – police identified him from the patterns further down his fingers. By the way, a note to criminals trying to avoid fingerprint detection by wearing gloves: leather and woven gloves can leave identifiable prints too!

The very first time someone was caught using fingerprint evidence was in Argentina in 1892 when a woman named Francisca Rojas claimed that one of her neighbours had attacked her home, killing two family members. Police matched bloody fingerprints on a doorframe to those of Rojas herself. Faced with the evidence, she confessed to the murders.

Fingerprints have proved crucial in numerous cases. In 1948, there was a kidnapping and murder in Blackburn, Lancashire, which was only solved because the killer had moved a bottle at the scene of the crime, leaving a print. The entire male population of the town was fingerprinted in order to track him down – number 46,253 turned out to be the culprit!

A similar operation was mounted a few years later, in 1955. A woman called Elizabeth Currell took her dog for a late evening walk across a golf course in Potter's Bar, Hertfordshire. She was attacked, and bravely fought her attacker off, but not until he'd fatally wounded her with the tee-iron which marked the course's seventeenth hole. After she was discovered the next day, police found just a small section of a palm print on the tee-iron.

It was very little evidence to go on! Police records in six counties were searched for a match, without success. A team of fifty-seven detectives, helped by twelve fingerprint experts, took prints from thousands of people who lived or worked in the area. Once again, careful forensic work finally resulted in a match: the murderer was a young clerk at the local town hall.

These days, police use various methods of Latent Fingerprint Identification, techniques for revealing prints which are either very faint or are on surfaces which can't normally be dusted for prints. The first time this sort of thing was done was in America in 1933, in the case of a kidnapped industrialist.

William Hamm, the president of a large company, was snatched outside his office in Minnesota by a gang. They demanded $100,000 for his release, the money was paid and the gang escaped. But not for long. Their fingerprints were discovered all over the ransom note! Paper was notoriously bad for finding prints on, and the crooks had thought they were safe.

The FBI Crime Lab had detected the prints using 'the silver nitrate method', which was brand new, state-of-the-art technology at the time. All fingerprints, even those you can't see with a magnifying glass, leave a residue of sweat, which contains sodium chloride, ordinary everyday salt. If you paint a solution of silver nitrate, a chemical which was then used in photography, over the area you think may contain a print, the silver nitrate reacts chemically with the sodium chloride. Result: when left in daylight, any previously invisible fingerprints turn white.

You can have a go at detecting your own fingerprints using the guide on page 227.

Another Three Cheers,
This Time for Anthropometry

Anthropometry, meaning 'the measurement of man', was developed by Alphone Bertillon in the 1870s. He was a clerk working in a police station in Paris and noticed that the chances of two grown adults being the same height were roughly four to one. Logically, he thought to himself, the same principle must apply to individual body parts too.

He developed a set of fourteen measurements – including circumference of head, length of fingers, length of foot and so on – which added together gave a set of figures that were almost as unique as a fingerprint. The chances of two people having the same dimensions were about two hundred million to one!

Bertillon's method, or Bertillonage as it was called, became popular across Europe as a means of making a positive ID on known criminals. However, it was a clunky system, which relied on using a huge number of index cards. As soon as fingerprinting became established, anthropometry was no more.

FOILED AGAIN!

One of the first times technology really counted in an investigation was way back in 1910, in catching Dr H. H. Crippen, a man whose slightly creepy surname became synonymous with evil and murder for decades afterwards.

Crippen was originally from America and wasn't a real doctor at all – he had a couple of bogus certificates in medicine and was involved in various medical scams and fakes for years. He was apparently a quiet, unassuming man, although he tended to dress in bright colours and had a reputation for being mean with money.

He was also thought of as a weasly little sponger by friends of his wife, Cora. She was a modestly successful singer in the London music halls, and was prone to temper tantrums, mostly aimed at her husband. She and Crippen weren't exactly the most devoted of married couples.

Crippen set himself up as a dentist. A young woman called Ethel was both his dental assistant and his girlfriend. Cora wasn't all that bothered about her husband's relationship with Ethel, because she had plenty of boyfriends of her own!

When Cora started spreading gossip about Ethel, Crippen decided he'd finally had enough of his wife. But instead of simply ending their marriage, he made up his mind to kill her.

A short time later, Cora's friends were suspicious when Crippen reported that Cora had returned to America without him. They were even more suspicious when he told them that she'd died over there. Inspector Dew of the CID investigated and Crippen told him that Cora had run off with one of her boyfriends. The Inspector believed him.

However, Crippen then aroused even more suspicion by suddenly disappearing from home, accompanied by Ethel. Inspector Dew returned to Crippen's house with a team of officers, and they found Cora's body buried in the cellar. She had been poisoned.

Crippen and Ethel might never have been caught if it hadn't been for the then brand-new invention of wireless telegraphy. The captain of the SS Montrose, a passenger ship heading for Canada, recognised Crippen from a newspaper photo. He'd been travelling as 'Mr Robinson' with Ethel, who was dressed as a boy.

The captain sent an urgent telegraph message: *Have strong suspicion that Crippen London cellar murderer and accomplice are among saloon passengers.* Police were ready and waiting when the ship docked. Crippen was the first criminal to be caught by radio!

These days, we're all familiar with the kind of high-tech police operation in which suspects are tracked from helicopters using infra-red or night-vision cameras. As new technologies are developed, police operations will become ever more complex.

EXHIBIT C:
SUDDENLY THEY HEARD A SCREAM!

THE WORLD OF
DETECTIVE FICTION

AS READERS OF MY case files will know, I'm a huge fan of detective stories. Name a famous detective story, and I've definitely read it. Probably. Anyway, the point is I've read a lot of them and I've read a lot about some of the people who wrote them (and how they did it). So here's a summary of what I've learnt.

Saxby

PART 1:

WRITING STORIES

What Is
a Detective Story?

A detective story is a story with a Detective Inspector in it, dum-dum! So-and-so of the Yard, or Some Guy in a Trenchcoat with a Whispery Voice.

Right?

No, not necessarily. A detective story doesn't *have* to include a police officer or a private eye or any official kind of investigator. It often does though. The detective in a detective story can be any character you like.

A detective story is not defined by *who* appears in it, but by *what happens*. These kinds of story have two distinct elements:

There is always a *mystery*.

Often (almost always, in fact) this mystery will involve a crime of some sort: 'Who stole my phone from my sports bag?', 'Who killed Sir Basil in the library with the spanner?', 'What is the sinister truth behind the pile of cash hidden in Auntie Gladys's wardrobe?' That sort of thing.

There is always an *investigation* into the mystery.

The puzzle is always unravelled, the problem is always worked out. This investigation can be carried out by any character – the point is that the investigation takes place.

There are different ways to tell a detective story. Provided that the *mystery* and the *investigation* are both there, the story itself can unfold in various ways. For example:

1. Lady Moneybag's ruby tiara is stolen! Nobody (including the readers of the story) knows who did it. Inspector Cleversausage turns up, examines the evidence, and reveals the truth. This is what you might call the standard, 'traditional' detective story plot.

2. Strange things happen. Our detective investigates various clues and gradually uncovers the cause of the mysterious goings-on. This plot turns things back-to-front: we follow the investigation and only discover the true nature of the mystery when we get to the end of the story.

3. A crime takes place. We, the readers, know exactly who did it and why, right from the start. The story is all about how the investigation proceeds, and how the good guys outwit the bad guys to uncover the truth.

There are lots of other forms that the plot of a detective story can take. As you read more stories, you discover more variations on the basic set-up of mystery and investigation.

Inside a lot of detective stories, you'll often find various 'plot devices'. A plot device is an object, an action or a character, which is written into the story for a specific reason: to provide vital information, perhaps, or to get the hero out of a tricky situation, or maybe to change the direction in which the story is going.

Some common detective story plot devices are:

Plot Device 1: The Red Herring

A red herring is a clue which looks like a clue but might not be a clue. Or maybe it is. Or maybe it's not . . .

Red herrings are things which may (or may not!) be deliberately misleading – elements which steer the reader and/or the fictional detective into following up clues which are irrelevant or fake. Or are they . . .?

(Why is it called a 'red herring'? Nobody really knows. It may come from hunting dogs in ye olden days that were deliberately led off the scent of prey using something stinky such as a herring. But it may be a phrase made up in the early nineteenth century by the writer William Cobbett. So the definition of 'red herring' could itself be . . . a red herring!)

Plot Device 2: Who Did It? Noooo Waaaaay!

One popular trick of the trade used by mystery writers is to make the least likely suspect the guilty one, so that it's a big surprise when you find out who committed the crime. For instance, you could have a story full of shifty-looking people dressed in stripy shirts and eye masks, yet the guilty one turns out to be . . . the tea lady!

Plot Device 3: A Sneaky Disguise

It's quite common in detective stories to find that a character isn't quite who you thought they were. Maybe Character A has a secret link to Character B that nobody knew about, or perhaps Character C and Character D turn out to be the same person in disguise. The simplest form of this plot device is to have the crime committed by a certain type of person (e.g. a very tall woman with long hair), and then reveal that it was actually a totally different type of person all along (e.g. a short man on stilts wearing a wig).

Plot Device 4: We're Trapped!

If a mystery writer wants to encourage the reader to turn detective and try to solve the mystery for themselves, one useful plot device is to have everything happen in some kind of enclosed situation. For example, in an isolated country house during a violent storm when nobody can get in or out, or on a boat in the middle of the ocean when nobody can get on or off. The idea is to have only a few characters, and so only a few suspects, and therefore make it an easier mystery for the reader to solve. This plot device most often turns up on TV or in movies, because it makes the drama cheaper to produce!

Plot Device 5: You Can't Trust 'Em, Inspector!

This is a particularly crafty plot device. Our detective talks to an important witness; the witness gives interesting information; the detective carries on with the investigation, using this information as crucial evidence. Then something happens which throws a spanner in the works: it turns out the witness might have had a reason to lie. Did they? Can our detective trust the evidence? Was the witness telling the truth or not?

There are many other plot devices. Sometimes one mystery is used to cover up a second. Sometimes absolutely nobody in a story can be trusted. And sometimes the old cliché 'the butler did it' turns out to be true!

Now we've worked out what a detective story is, and what sort of things appear in it, it's time to dive into the murky waters of mystery both real and imaginary . . .

OMG!
THE BUTLER DID IT!

Almost all authors **PLAN** their stories very carefully (detective story authors, at least) and rarely begin writing before everything has been thought out.

Phase 1: Do the Basics (like they tell you at school!)

This applies to any story you might want to write. Ask yourself four questions. You don't need to answer them in this order, but they must all be answered:

What's the SETTING for your story? *WHERE* will it take place, and *WHEN*? An easy choice, really, since you can set stories anywhere. However, bear in mind the events you want to happen in the story – if it includes people chatting on their smartphones, then clearly you can't set your story during Elizabethan times!

What CHARACTERS will you include? Trickier than it looks – your characters must suit your story (e.g. If you want to write a Hardboiled detective thriller, probably best not to include that savage man-eating elephant you just thought up. He won't fit in. Save him for another story, one which is more zoological). All your characters must play a proper part in the story – too few characters and the story may become dull, too many and the story may become confused. Be careful **WHO** you put in your story.

What is the PLOT of your story? Very tricky, especially with a detective story. Eveything must be worked out, everything must make sense. You must not only know *WHAT* is happening in your story at all times, but also *WHY* it is happening. (TOP TIP: If you get stuck when working out a plot, ask yourself *why* you're stuck – take a step back and examine the plot for contradictions or gaps.)

What is the STYLE of your story? Stories can be funny, sad, scary, dramatic, romantic, atmospheric . . . It's often possible to tell the same story in a number of different styles. Decide *HOW* you want to tell your story.

Phase 2: Learn from the Greats

There are no firm rules when it comes to sitting down and putting your detective story on paper. But if you read about the lives of your favourite mystery writers, it's possible to find things in common. For example:

Keep a notebook. Always very useful. You never know when inspiration will strike. Jot down whatever interests you – names, ideas, things you see, things you hear. Agatha Christie kept four or five notebooks going at once; she often used people she saw on buses as characters in her books.

Work backwards. When planning a detective story, one extremely handy tip is to start at the solving of the mystery and work your way back. Suppose your story involves a bank robbery: work out how the bad guys managed to smuggle a million gold bars out of the vault FIRST, and THEN go back and decide how the crime is discovered at the start of the story. (Try it. It's much harder the 'normal' way around!)

Get to the point. Another thing Agatha Christie (and others) did was to write in very straightforward language, using short sentences and everyday words. This helped readers whizz through her books! Christie also kept descriptive sections towards the beginning of her stories, so that readers could race through the last pages and discover who did it even faster.

<u>Phase 3: Keep Going</u>

Even the most experienced writers can find creating a completed story very hard work.

Don't give up. It doesn't matter how long it takes, see your story through to the end.

Don't worry if you need to go back and change things. A lot of writers say that it's the re-writing of a story which produces the best results!

Read! There's barely a writer in the world who isn't a big reader. Reading is the best way to improve your writing – you never stop learning from great writers!

PART 2:

READING STORIES

A Brief Timeline
of Detective Stories

(For more information,
see the sections on each individual writer.)

1841   Edgar Allan Poe's *Murders in the Rue Morgue*

1868   Wilkie Collins's *The Moonstone*

1887   Sir Arthur Conan Doyle's first Sherlock
           Holmes story, *A Study in Scarlet*

1920s / Detective stories split into two distinct styles
1930s

The 'Whodunit'   The 'Hardboiled'
puzzle   thriller
e.g. the works of   e.g. the works of
Agatha Christie   Raymond Chandler

1960s   The two styles merge – this mix of mystery and
onward   psychology is still going strong today.

EDGAR ALLAN POE

The American writer Edgar Allan Poe invented the detective story in 1841. Simple as that.

Before that, there had been a few books which included one or two elements of detective fiction, but it wasn't until Edgar Allan Poe wrote his short story *Murders in the Rue Morgue* that the *mystery* and *investigation* set-up of the detective story (see page 144) came together for the very first time.

His Early Life

Poe was born in Boston, north-east USA, in 1809. Both his mother and father were stage performers (his mother was pretty good at it, his father much less so). They were also very poor.

When Poe was two years old, his mother left his father and took him and his brother and sister to live almost five hundred miles away in Virginia. Then she died. Poe was split up from his siblings and ended up in the care of a couple called John and Frances Allan. Young Edgar Poe thus became young Edgar Allan Poe.

He was given a decent education and was quite an athlete as a teenager. However, he was often bullied at school because his parents were in the theatre (at that time, being a performer was seen as a rather shameful career choice). He was also bullied for the opposite reason – because he was looked after by the Allans and not his parents! The poor guy just couldn't win!

From Bad to Worse

Bad luck and poverty seemed to haunt him. He enrolled in the University of Virginia but dropped out when he got badly into debt and a girl he secretly liked got engaged to another man. Partly, his problems were down to his own bad habits: he gambled money away, and the older he got the more alcohol he drank.

He had a short but surprisingly successful time in the army, which he joined at the age of 18 under the fake name Edgar Perry. He rose to the rank of Sergeant Major, and ended up at the highly prestigious West Point Military Academy in 1830.

However, his bad habits soon got him thrown out of West Point. He got married and went to live with his aunt in Philadelphia, not far from New York.

By now he'd been writing poetry for a while and after his first couple of poetry collections were published he branched out into short stories, book reviews and articles on literature, which he wrote for various different magazines. He was even a magazine editor for a while, but once again his bad habits put an end to any long-term plans he might have had.

His Stories

Edgar Allan Poe was not what's called a 'prolific' writer – he didn't write that much stuff during his lifetime. In fact, all his stories and poems fit comfortably into one chunky paperback today. However, his stories had a huge impact on writers who came after him, and his work has an important place in the history of literature.

He wrote a number of brilliantly creepy stories such as *The Fall of the House of Usher*, *The Black Cat* and *The Pit and the Pendulum*, and a mournful poem called *The Raven* which became a big hit at the time. These stories were so effective because he wove a lot of his own fears and unhappiness into them. One of them, an allegory about disease called *Masque of the Red Death*, was written while Philadelphia was in the middle of a cholera outbreak. (An allegory is a story or poem with a deliberate second meaning 'underneath' the story.) Poe's wife had also recently contracted tuberculosis, which would gradually destroy her health and finally kill her five years later. (More tragedy for the Poe family.) Poe also wrote one or two stories which can be seen as early experiments in science fiction.

The World's First Detective Stories

In 1841, Poe wrote a story called *Murders in the Rue Morgue*. It was set in Paris and featured a couple of gruesome and baffling murders. It also featured a character called C. Auguste Dupin, a nobleman obsessed with logic, detail and deduction – the first ever fictional detective!

The story wasn't actually meant to be the first of its kind. Poe didn't get up one morning and say, 'Today I'm going to invent a whole new style of fiction'. He simply set out to write an interesting and thought-provoking story. It just so happened that *Murders in the Rue Morgue* brought the mystery and investigation formula into focus for the very first time.

Poe couldn't even call it a 'detective story' – the word 'detective' didn't even exist at the time! The first real-life detective started work the following year, 1842 (see page

105). Poe called it a 'tale of ratiocination' (in other words, a tale of logical deduction).

There were only two more short stories featuring Auguste Dupin, *The Mystery of Marie Roget* and *The Purloined Letter*. These three stories – just three! – started off the entire detective story genre.

Real-Life Mystery

One strange aspect of Edgar Allan Poe's life story is the mystery surrounding his death. In October 1849, he was discovered, half conscious and extremely ill, lying in the middle of the street in Baltimore, miles from his home.

He couldn't explain how he'd got there or why he was in such a terrible state. He was taken to the local hospital. Here, he lay in a fever for three days and then died. The circumstances of his death have never been properly explained. Poe's own life turned into something he might have written into one of his Auguste Dupin stories!

A Good Read?

Edgar Allan Poe's stories are still read and enjoyed today. They can make quite difficult reading – they often include a lot of long and unusual words – but they're well worth tackling (perhaps with a dictionary to hand, or perhaps in audiobook form!).

WILKIE COLLINS

About twenty years after Edgar Allan Poe wrote the very first short detective stories along came the first detective novel: *The Moonstone*. This was the first book we could still read today and recognise as detective fiction, because it's got all the right elements in the story: a mystery, a police detective, lots of plot twists and turns, people creeping about in the dark, the lot.

An Unusual Child

The Moonstone was written by an English author called Wilkie Collins. In the 1860s and 1870s, he was second only to Charles Dickens in terms of popularity as a writer.

Collins was born in London in 1824 and was the son of a well-known landscape artist, William Collins. He was brought up in relative wealth and lived with his family in Italy and France for a couple of years, but he was always a sickly kid. He was born with a slightly deformed skull, which made his head look rather large and bulging, and he had hands and feet which were unusually small.

An Unusual Adult

When he grew up, he was unconventional in other ways. He would often dress in a flamboyant style, he loved his food and he was very fond of overseas travel. He never married but lived – on and off – with two women. He had three children with one of them.

Today, living arrangements like that are nothing very remarkable, but in Victorian times they were scandalous! Collins would often have to pretend one of the women was his wife, or his housekeeper, to stop gossip spreading.

An Unusual Writer

Wilkie Collins's first jobs were working for a tea merchant (which he hated), and as a lawyer (which he was also far from keen on, although lawyers turn up in quite a few of his books). His first couple of novels were quite well received, but his career began to soar after a friend with the peculiar name Augustus Egg introduced him to Charles Dickens.

Dickens and Collins became great friends. They would read and criticise each other's work, which helped both of them improve their writing.

Collins had a HUGE hit in 1860 with a novel called *The Woman in White*. This was what the Victorians called a 'sensation' novel, one full of drama and scandal and fluttery Victorian ladies. *The Woman in White* became the biggest selling book of the nineteenth century – and it's still a darn good read today!

Read That, Worn the T-Shirt

We think of merchandising – products linked to movies and TV series – as a modern idea, but it isn't. *The Woman in White* was such a smash hit that the shops were soon full of *Woman in White* cloaks, *Woman in White* bonnets, *Woman in White* perfume . . . there was even a *Woman in White* waltz!

An Unusual Book

The Moonstone was another of Collins's immensely popular 'sensation' novels. He didn't set out to create the first detective novel, of course. He simply wanted to write an exciting story that his readers would enjoy. It just so happened that the elements which went into *The Moonstone* set the tone for all the detective stories which would follow.

One of the great crime writers of the early twentieth century, Dorothy L. Sayers, described *The Moonstone* as 'probably the finest detective story ever written', although for some reason Collins's old mate Dickens didn't think it was one of his best. The book was almost as big a hit as *The Woman in White* – readers would wait in crowds outside the publisher's offices for the latest instalment to arrive (like most Victorian novels, it was first printed in parts in a magazine).

After *The Moonstone*

Wilkie Collins was a sickly child, and he became a sickly adult. He suffered for many years from what he called 'rheumatic gout', which was probably a form of arthritis (painful and swollen joints), and his eyesight was poor.

The medicines and painkillers available in those days were very dangerous by today's standards, and Collins quickly became addicted to them. The poor man often suffered the delusion that he was being followed around by an identical twin. It's no wonder that horrible side-effects like that and characters with odd medical problems also crop up regularly in his novels.

Collins's books of the 1870s and 1880s weren't as good as his earlier works, partly because of his ever-worsening illness. He died in 1889, having lived almost his whole life in the Marylebone area of London where he was born.

The First of Its Kind: The Story of The Moonstone

Young Rachel Verinder receives an amazing birthday gift: a huge diamond, The Moonstone, left to her in the will of her disreputable uncle. Little does she know that it's been stolen from its rightful home in India, and that those whose job it was to guard it will stop at nothing to get it back.

Rachel wears the diamond at her birthday party. That night, she carefully hides it away in her room. The next morning . . . it's gone!

Sergeant Cuff, a famous police detective, investigates the case. Why have three mysterious Indian travelling showmen been seen near the house? What does the strange behaviour of Rosanna the housemaid signify? Is Rachel herself involved in the diamond's disappearance?

Clues point this way and that, until the shocking truth is discovered.

SIR ARTHUR CONAN DOYLE

The Victorian sleuth Sherlock Holmes is the most famous fictional detective of all time, possibly the most famous fictional character of any kind. You might say he was the Harry Potter of his day – a character with millions of fans all over the world.

Holmes was created by the Scottish writer Arthur Conan Doyle, who also wrote a large number of non-Holmes stories, novels and non-fiction articles during his lifetime. Conan Doyle was one of ten children, whose Irish mum could trace her family back to the Middle Ages. This may be one reason Doyle grew up with a passion for history!

The Real-Life Holmes

He studied medicine in Edinburgh at the end of the 1870s, and it was while he was there that he met the man who would become part of the inspiration for Sherlock Holmes. One of Doyle's tutors was Dr Joseph Bell, who had an impressive ability to observe and deduce things about his patients. Dr Bell could look strangers up and down and immediately tell them, to their complete astonishment, all sorts of facts about themselves. Bell himself considered this no more than an amusing trick, but when Conan Doyle was thinking about writing the first Holmes story – years later – he thought back to his old tutor and realised that a character with Bell's quick-witted observational skills would make an ideal detective.

Real-Life Inspiration

Sherlock Holmes wasn't the only Conan Doyle character inspired by a real person. Another of Doyle's tutors at Edinburgh was Professor Rutherford, whose huge beard and booming voice became part of Professor Challenger, hero of *The Lost World* and other stories.

Conan Doyle: Writer, Sportsman, Campaigner

Conan Doyle was a very busy guy: he had a lifelong love of sport and was particularly good at cricket and golf; he twice stood for parliament (but wasn't elected); he served as an army medic during the Boer War in South Africa; he was a campaigner against miscarriages of justice (cases in which people were wrongly convicted of a crime); and on top of all that, he was an enthusiastic amateur photographer. And a doctor. And an author.

After his medical studies, and a spell as a ship's medic, Conan Doyle became what would now be called a GP, a family doctor, first in Plymouth and then in Southsea. Although his practice was fairly successful, he found he had time on his hands during the working day, in between seeing patients. Being a person who liked to be busy, he filled the time with writing, and one of the stories he wrote was the first Sherlock Holmes adventure, called *A Study in Scarlet*.

Doyle and Holmes

Sherlock Holmes was a huge hit with readers. However, he wasn't a big hit with Conan Doyle himself. Everything became so focused on Holmes, with readers and publishers demanding new stories, that Conan Doyle found himself with little time for writing anything else.

He considered his Holmes stories to be nothing more

than light, unimportant stuff. He wanted to get on with epic, historical novels, and the thought that he might only be remembered for Sherlock Holmes was something which he found deeply frustrating.

Doyle soon came to feel trapped by Holmes. One way in which you can see this coming out in the stories is Doyle's disregard for detail. For example, Holmes's sidekick Dr Watson is described as having a war wound, but in some stories that wound is in his shoulder, and in others it's in his leg! Holmes's arch-enemy Professor Moriarty appears in two stories, but in both of those stories Dr Watson claims it's the first time he's encountered him.

Holmes Dies . . . Or Does He?

Eventually, Conan Doyle got so fed up of Sherlock Holmes that he decided to kill him off. So, in a story called *The Final Problem*, he had Holmes fall to his death over a waterfall.

Readers were appalled! Some people took to wearing a black band around their arm, just as they would have done if a real person had died. Instead of taking the pressure off, Doyle found that Holmes's death only increased readers' cries for more stories! After a few years, Conan Doyle finally gave in and brought Sherlock Holmes back.

Opposites

One interesting aspect of the Holmes/Doyle story is the way that Sherlock Holmes and his creator were total opposites. Holmes is a person who values logic and reason above all else, but Arthur Conan Doyle was someone who literally believed in fairies.

There was a very famous incident surrounding some photos, apparently showing real fairies, taken by a couple of young girls in a village called Cottingley (it's too long a story to get into here and now – look up 'Cottingley fairies' if you'd like to know more). The photos were, of course, fake, but Conan Doyle was amongst those who declared the pictures to be real. He even wrote a book about the case in 1922 called *The Coming of the Fairies*.

Over the course of his life, Conan Doyle also became more and more interested in Spiritualism (contacting the dead, getting messages from spirits, that sort of thing). Sherlock Holmes would have laughed in his face!

Conan Doyle's support for such issues damaged his reputation as a serious campaigner. It also led to a bitter public battle of words with the American showman and magician Harry Houdini, who was originally a great friend of Conan Doyle's but who was on a personal crusade to show spiritualists as fakes and con-men.

Arthur Conan Doyle died in 1930. Sherlock Holmes

may well live forever. He certainly did more than any other character to turn detective stories into the world-wide popular reading they still are today.

Sherlock Holmes: The Books

A Study in Scarlet (novel, 1887)

The Sign of the Four (novel, 1890)

The Adventures of Sherlock Holmes (short stories, 1892)

The Memoirs of Sherlock Holmes (short stories, 1894)

The Hound of the Baskervilles (novel, 1902)

The Return of Sherlock Holmes (short stories, 1905)

The Valley of Fear (novel, 1915)

His Last Bow (short stories, 1917)

The Case-Book of Sherlock Holmes (short stories, 1927)

THE 'GOLDEN AGE' OF DETECTIVE FICTION

In complete contrast to the 'Hardboiled' style of detective story (see page 183), there was what's been called the 'Golden Age' of crime fiction. This was a style of story mostly used by English writers between the First and Second World Wars.

While Hardboiled writers tried to present gritty and realistic stories, Golden Age writers usually set their mysteries in a rather old fashioned world. A Golden Age story is one in which there's often a slightly spooky country house, where household servants glide around behind upper class characters, and where the murder of old Mr What's-his-name is simply one strand in a dastardly web of intrigue and lies.

Golden Age stories are the ones in which you'll generally find a selection of familiar murder mystery characters – a few lords and ladies, a couple of butlers and maids, perhaps a rich businessman or a glamorous young woman lounging on a sofa. These are stories which revolve around a *puzzle*, not around the characters. They are about how the detective goes about discovering the truth, and about whether the reader can also work out who did it.

Because of the way these stories concentrate on the plot rather than on the characters, Golden Age mysteries often have fiendishly complicated solutions! The kind of criss-crossing network of clues and evidence you find in a Golden Age story is another thing which shows that they're not terribly worried about being realistic, in the sense that you'd hardly ever find such a complex (and neatly concluded!) set of events in real life.

It's sometimes argued that Golden Age detective fiction became popular because, during the 1920s and 1930s, the real world was one in which the horrors of the First World War were still being felt, and in which there was a great deal of political and economic turmoil. The cosy, logical world of the detective story was an entertaining retreat for readers, in the same way as some TV series today are described as 'escapist'.

The most widely read Golden Age author was – no prizes for guessing! – Agatha Christie, but there was a long line of writers creating stories in the same basic style. In fact, Golden Age plots became so much of a game between writer and reader that, in 1929, the crime writer Ronald Knox wrote down a set of rules that all such stories ought to stick to. These included:

1. *Not more than one secret room or passage is allowable.*

2. *No hitherto undiscovered poisons may be used, nor any appliance which will need a long scientific explanation at the end.* (No home-made ray guns, etc!)

3. *All supernatural or preternatural agencies . . .* (ghosts, vampires etc) *. . . are ruled out as a matter of course.*

4. *No accident must ever help the detective, nor must he ever have an unaccountable intuition which proves to be right.* (In other words, he must work it all out for himself!)

5. *The detective himself must not commit the crime.*

Although Knox wasn't being totally serious, these rules make pretty good guidelines for anyone writing a Golden Age-type story, even today.

Reading List: Some Favourite Golden Agers

Writer	Most popular detective
Margery Allingham	Albert Campion, an 'unofficial' investigator with links to Scotland Yard
Ngaio Marsh (pronounced Nye-Oh)	Roderick Alleyn, a CID police detective
Dorothy L. Sayers	Lord Peter Wimsey, an amateur sleuth
Georges Simenon	Maigret, a French police inspector
Josephine Tey	Inspector Alan Grant of Scotland Yard
G. K. Chesterton	Father Brown, a priest
John Dickson Carr	Dr Gideon Fell, another amateur sleuth (who was based on G. K. Chesterton!)

AGATHA CHRISTIE

Agatha Christie, born Agatha Miller in 1890 (Christie was the surname of her first husband), remains one of the world's most popular authors ever.

Like a lot of girls at that time, she never went to school and was taught by her mum and the occasional private tutor. Not that she remained uneducated: she'd taught herself to read by the time she was five years old!

Imaginary Friends

Her brother and sister were older than her and were away from home from most of the time, so Agatha had a lonely childhood in which she had to entertain herself.

There were few children living near the family's large house in Devon, and in any case Agatha was a very shy girl.

As a result, she developed a vivid imagination, inventing characters to share her games with. At the age of nine she made up all her own school friends – including one or two fellow 'pupils' she really didn't like!

She travelled abroad with her mother, something which gave her a lifelong love of overseas explorations, and when she was sixteen she was sent to Paris for two years to study singing and the piano. She was an excellent pianist and might have had a career in music, had it not been for her extreme shyness when it came to performing.

Stories

Agatha had always been encouraged to create stories and poems, and as she grew up she thought about maybe, possibly, one day having a go at writing a book. Then, a conversation with her sister Madge in 1915 marked a turning point for Agatha.

The sisters had been discussing the crime novel *The Mystery of the Yellow Room* by Gaston Leroux. Agatha said she'd like to write a detective story. Madge told her she'd be hopeless at it. From that moment on, Agatha was determined to get a crime novel written and published! Her first book, *The Mysterious Affair at Styles*, finally appeared in 1920.

Some Background Information

During World War I, Agatha worked as a nurse looking after wounded troops. It was a job she enjoyed, and while she was at the Red Cross Torbay Hospital she learnt a great deal about medicines and in particular about poisons. This knowledge would be very valuable to her in her later writing – poisons feature prominently in her crime stories. In fact, she was such an expert on poisons that there were at least two occasions when real-life doctors were able to diagnose cases of poisoning based on what they'd read in an Agatha Christie mystery!

Christie often used bits of real life as inspiration for her stories. For example, her detective Hercule Poirot was made a Belgian because there were a lot of Belgian refugees in the UK at the time, and the measles epidemic which features in the book *The Mirror Crack'd* was something that was really happening as she wrote the story (see also the Lindbergh case, page 74).

Poirot and Marple

Unlike many crime writers, Agatha Christie created

more than one fictional detective. Hercule Poirot and Miss Marple are her two most famous.

Poirot, the Belgian private eye, is a neatly dressed and rather fussy man, who relies on what he calls 'the little grey cells' (in other words, his brain) to help him solve the case. Miss Jane Marple is, essentially, just a nosy old lady, who happens to be a sharp observer of human behaviour. Christie based her partly on her own grandmother.

Like Arthur Conan Doyle and Sherlock Holmes (see page 166), Christie became very tired of Poirot, but unlike Doyle she was happy to keep writing about a character her readers loved. She was familiar with Conan Doyle's books and deliberately gave the Poirot stories a similar feel: an eccentric detective, a slightly dim sidekick (while Holmes had Watson, she created a chap called Hastings for Poirot), a bumbling police official (Inspector Lestrade for Holmes, Chief Inspector Japp for Poirot), even a barely-seen older brother who works for the government (Mycroft for Holmes, Achille for Poirot – although Achille may have been a figment of Hercule Poirot's imagination!).

Also Starring . . .

Some of Christie's other detectives were:
* Tuppence and Tommy Beresford, who often got mixed up in the world of spies.
* Superintendent Battle, a police detective.
* Mrs Ariadne Oliver, a mystery writer based on Christie herself.
* The mysterious Harley Quin and Mr Satterthwaite (no, nothing to do with Batman!).
* Parker Pyne, who didn't so much investigate cases as re-arrange them.

Quite a lot of Christie's characters would pop up in each other's stories. The only two detectives who never met were Poirot and Miss Marple.

A Real Mystery

Agatha Christie was a private person who – apart from her travels abroad – liked to live a quiet life. However, there is one mysterious incident which lurks in her life story: towards the end of 1926, by which time she was already very famous as a writer, she vanished for almost two weeks. She left her home in Berkshire, leaving a note for her secretary saying she was going to Yorkshire.

But no trace of her could be found. The police and public searched the entire country, but to no avail. Her disappearance was headline news in many parts of the world. Eleven days later, she was finally discovered at a hotel in Harrogate, where she'd been staying under a false name.

She claimed to have amnesia (memory loss) and couldn't, or wouldn't, explain what had happened. A lot of people thought it had all been a publicity stunt, which it almost certainly wasn't, and were angry with her for wasting everyone's time.

The truth has never been revealed. The most likely explanation is that Christie was so upset over the ending of her first marriage, and the recent death of her mother, that she simply had to get away for a while. But when she wrote her autobiography, many years later, she never once mentioned those two weeks, and there are still a number of unanswered questions relating to the incident.

Last Books

During World War II, Christie wrote the final adventures of Poirot and Miss Marple, *Curtain* and *Sleeping Murder*. However, she locked them away in a bank vault, intending that they should only be published once she was sure she'd write no more books. *Curtain* was finally published in 1975, and *Sleeping Murder* came out in 1976, shortly after Agatha Christie's death.

Agatha Christie in Numbers

Christie wrote **66 novels**,
13 plays and
154 short stories.

Her work has been translated into over
50 languages
published in over **70 countries**,
and has sold over **2 BILLION copies**.

There have been more than **60 movies**, and
more than **100 TV adaptations** of her books.

Her play *The Mousetrap* has run for over
24,000 performances
in one London theatre alone.

THE HARDBOILED
DETECTIVE STORY

There's a HUGE difference between the kind of detective stories classified as 'Golden Age' (see page 172), and the kind of detective stories classified as 'Hardboiled'. If you look at the timeline on page 155, you'll see that detective fiction splits during the 1920s and 1930s into two very distinct types of story.

Here's an interesting fact: of the Golden Age writers, almost all of the most successful were English, and almost all were women. Of the Hardboiled writers, almost all the most successful were American, and almost all were men.

While Golden Age stories tend to emphasise *plot* and *puzzles*, Hardboiled stories tend to emphasise *action* and *psychology* (psychology in the sense of the motives and lifestyles lurking behind the work of the detective). Golden Age stories often have country settings, Hardboiled stories almost always have urban, inner-city settings. The good guys in Golden Age stories generally rely on their brains, while the good guys in Hardboiled stories generally rely on being tough and streetwise.

> Why are they called 'Hardboiled'? Simply because, just like an egg, a Hardboiled story is going to be harder and tougher than one that's soft and runny!

Hardboiled detective stories became enormously popular from the 1920s onward. In 1921 (the year after Agatha Christie's first book was published), a magazine called *Black Mask* appeared on news-stands in America. *Black Mask*, which featured nothing but detective stories every month, would have a very big influence on the history of crime fiction. It introduced Hardboiled stories to an ever increasing audience of readers, and it was also the first publication to feature work by many of the great Hardboiled writers, most notably Dashiell Hammett and Raymond Chandler.

Black Mask was what's called a pulp magazine. At that time, before TV, the internet or video games, many Americans (and Europeans!) enjoyed reading monthly magazine collections of short stories. Competition between these magazines was fierce. They needed to be as cheaply produced as possible (few people ever kept them once they'd been read), so they were printed on very low quality wood-pulp paper. Pulp magazines featuring science-fiction stories and Western adventures were just as popular as those featuring detective fiction.

Black Mask was so successful that lots of other magazines copied it. Some of *Black Mask*'s rivals were pretty good, and some were pretty rubbish. But they all fought for the attention of readers with exciting-sounding titles and dramatic front covers.

There were many writers of Hardboiled stories, most of them working for very little money (the pulp magazines would pay them around one or two cents per word for their work). The only way they could earn a living was to churn out loads and loads of stories. Result: some really great stories, but an awful lot of badly written stories too!

Despite this, writers such as Carroll John Daly (who more or less invented the basic Hardboiled style),

James M. Cain, Cornell Woolrich and Erle Stanley Gardner managed to write stories that are still considered really good today.

> Here's another interesting fact: Hardboiled stories regularly used a writing style that hadn't often been seen before in detective fiction: first person narrative. In other words, they would often say 'I investigated the crime scene' instead of 'The detective investigated the crime scene' – one of the characters narrated the story. Agatha Christie had used a first person narrator before, but it was very uncommon until the pulps came along.

Besides Raymond Chandler (see page 194), perhaps the best and most influential Hardboiled writer was Dashiell Hammett. He grew up in Philadelphia and Baltimore (Edgar Allan Poe's old haunts!) and left school at the age of thirteen. He fought in World War I and – despite the fact that by then he had tuberculosis – fought in World War II as well.

His most famous creation is the private eye Sam Spade, who appeared in Hammett's most famous book, *The Maltese Falcon*. But Hammett wrote a long list of excellent novels and short story collections, in a straight-to-the-point style which is a must-read for anyone who wants to find out what Hardboiled detective stories are all about.

A GLOSSARY
OF HARDBOILED
SLANG

*Or, How to Sound Like a Character
from a Black Mask Story*

(Readers are advised not to attempt speaking any of the following words without first putting on a slightly comical accent a bit like the gangsters in Looney Tunes cartoons, or Mayor Quimby in *The Simpsons*.)

People

Newshawk	Newspaper reporter
Newsie	Newspaper seller
Mug/rube/sap	Idiot, fool, easy target

A Glossary of Hardboiled Slang

Broad / dame / doll	Woman
Moll	Girlfriend
Croaker	Doctor (nothing to do with frogs!)
Mouthpiece / shyster	Lawyer
Fink / stool-pigeon / stoolie	Informant, one who rats (see below)
Highbinder	A corrupt official

Places

Joint	A general word for a place
Clip joint	Bar or club which charges high prices or cheats customers
Dive	A joint with a bad reputation
Speakeasy	Any illegal bar
Burg	Town
Flop house	Cheap or seedy hotel
Hash house	Cheap or seedy restaurant

Money and Valuables

Dough/jack	Money
Two bits	Twenty-five cents
Berries	Dollars
Five-spot/fin	Five dollars
Sawbuck	Ten dollars
Century/'c'/yard	One hundred dollars
Madison portrait	Five hundred dollars
Grand/large	One thousand dollars
Ice	Diamonds
Marbles	Pearls

Busy, Busy, Busy . . .

To paste/ bop/ sock	To punch
To brace	To grab
To dry-gulch	To knock out
To grab air	To raise your hands (in surrender)
To finger	To identify (in the sense of betraying, being a stoolie)
To pack iron/wear iron	Carry a gun
To crash out/cop the sneak/take it on the lam	To escape, go on the run

To drift/fade/take a powder/take the air	To go into hiding
To burn/throw metal/throw lead/drill	To shoot, fire a gun
To blow down/bump/bop/croak/rub out	To kill
To kick off/catch the big one/wear a Chicago overcoat	To die

It's the Cops!

Bracelets/nippers/cuffs	Handcuffs
To clamp/nab/pinch	To arrest
Big house/can/cooler	Prison
Buzzer	Police badge
Clubhouse	Police station
Bull/cop/john/flatty	Police officer
Gumshoe/shamus/dick/gum-heel/snooper	Private detective
Ticket	Private detective's licence
Two-time loser	Criminal who's been convicted twice
Rap	Criminal charge (a rap-sheet is a criminal record)

It's the Bad Guys!

Goon/hood/punk/hoodlum	Any criminal thug
Dropper/hatchetman/torpedo/triggerman	A hired gunman
Con	Anyone with a criminal record
Bird-guy/yegg/yeggman/peterman	Safe-cracker
Dip	Pickpocket
Yap	Petty crook
Grifter	Con-man, fraudster
Bunco/flimflam	Con-trick, fraud, swindle
To gyp/nick/trim	To cheat, con
To shake down	To obtain by force (also means to search)
Ringer	A fake
Knockover/heist	Raid, theft or robbery
Snatch	Kidnapping
Mob	Gang
Pill/lug	Bullet
Bean-shooter/gat/heat/heater/roscoe/cannon	Gun

Vocabulary for Everyday Conversations

Hack	Taxi
Heap	Car
Meat wagon	Ambulance
Bang-tail/pony	Racehorse
To beef	To grumble
To rat/squeal	To give information to the police
Rats and mice	Dice
Crap game/craps	Any dice game (nothing to do with whether it's any good or not!)
Pug	Boxer
Dope	Information
Bum steer	Something worthless
Busted flush	A complete failure
Bunk/hooey	Nonsense, rubbish
Cinch	Easy (still used today!)
Nix	No, nothing
Youse	Plural of 'you'
Stiff	Dead body
Noggin/noodle	Head
To shoot the works	To risk all (also means to tell the truth)

RAYMOND CHANDLER

An American Writer?

Raymond Chandler is regarded as one of the best crime writers ever. He's thought of as a very American author, because his stories are all set there, but he spent a large section of his early life in Europe.

He was born in Chicago in 1888 but moved to England as a child after his parents divorced. He went to Dulwich College, an English public school, and he also studied in France and Germany. Once he left school, he tried composing romantic poetry, but he realised he wasn't all that good at it. He returned to the States in 1912, by which time he spoke in a rather posh, upper class English accent!

Any Sort of Writer?

As a young man, up to the early 1930s, he did all sorts of different jobs. For a while he was in the Canadian Army and during World War I he flew fighter aircraft for the British. He took up a career in the American oil industry, and ended up as Vice-President of the Dabney Oil Syndicate. However, his heart was never really in the job, and in 1932 he was sacked.

A Detective Writer!

It was only in his forties that he began to write crime and mystery short stories, mostly for the influential pulp magazine *Black Mask*.

Detective stories might have seemed a strange choice of subject matter for him. Why? Because most crime writers in America at that time had worked in the police or law enforcement in some way. For example, Dashiell Hammett (see page 186) had been a private eye with the Pinkerton detective agency. Raymond Chandler had no knowledge of the subject at all. He had to catch up by reading a lot of crime fiction, to find out what people were writing about, and he studied every book on criminology and police methods he could get his hands on.

His first published story, called *Blackmailers Don't Shoot*, appeared in *Black Mask* at the end of 1933. After that, he spent all his time writing. However, like Edgar Allan Poe (see page 156), he wasn't an author who wrote loads of stories. In fact, between 1933 and 1939 he only completed nineteen stories. One of them *Killer in the Rain*, became the basis of his first novel, entitled *The Big Sleep*. This was the story that introduced his most famous creation, the private eye Philip Marlowe.

Hang On a Minute . . .

Why did Raymond Chandler start writing crime stories when he'd never been interested in them before?

Chandler had strong feelings about justice and the law. His Philip Marlowe novels, set in 1930s, Los Angeles, are filled with an atmosphere of sleaze and corruption which seeps through every level of society. In these stories, the detective Marlowe is almost a knight-in-shining-armour figure (not literally, of course, he wore a lot of long coats and wide-brimmed hats!). Marlowe is portrayed as one decent, morally good man in a world full of crooks and low-lifes.

Chandler's deep sense of fair play made him angry whenever he saw innocent people losing out to villains in real life. He intensely disliked the kind of underhand, sneaky double-dealing that went on in business and politics. Both during his time in the oil industry and after he moved to Los Angeles, he felt he was surrounded by injustice and greed.

He wrote crime stories because, as he put it, they were 'the most honest'. In his fictional world, he could right wrongs and defend the truth. His stories are always about honourable people struggling against a dishonourable world.

A Grumpy Writer?

His anger at greed and injustice often spilt out of his stories and into his real life. For example, he would go bananas at the 'blood-sucking leeches' who published his books because he didn't want to split his earnings with them (which was very unfair of him!). In later life he wrote movie scripts in Hollywood, and he absolutely hated the whole movie-making system.

The slow speed at which he wrote meant he completed only six Philip Marlowe mysteries, alongside his short stories and screenplays for films such as *Double Indemnity* and *The Blue Dahlia*. A large number of planned projects ended up abandoned – he simply never got around to them.

In the last few years of his life he suffered ill health and travelled between Europe and America, becoming ever more bad-tempered. He died in California in 1959, leaving another unfinished project, a Marlowe novel called (how's this for a weird title) *Poodle Spring*.

Raymond Chandler steered the detective novel in entirely new directions. His books were amongst the first to make readers think about how crime stories might relate to real life and to the way people really live. He influenced the detective story so much that even now, many decades later, there are echoes of the Chandler writing style and the Chandler sense of justice in almost any tough, streetwise fictional sleuth.

EXHIBIT D:
Do It Yourself

How To Be a Brilliant Schoolkid Detective

IF YOU WANT TO be a brilliant schoolkid detective, like me, there are two things you must have: a razor-sharp mind and a pen that works. And a notebook, of course, to go with the pen. Er, that's three things. OK, there are three things all brilliant schoolkid detectives need: a razor-sharp mind, a pen that works and a notebook. And fearlessness, because sometimes you can end up in tricky situations. Hang on, that's four things. Hmm. OK, let's just say that you need to be ready for anything. The stuff that follows is all about being ready for anything.

Saxby

YOUR
DETECTIVE TOOLKIT

You're on the case! You're at the crime scene! Your astonishing deductive powers stand ready ('cos they're attached to your brain), but what sort of kit will you need, in order to make best use of them? What equipment should you have with you at all times?

Notepad and Pen
Obvious, really! A thousand and one uses: crime scene sketches, witness statements, facts and figures, your own thoughts on the case, etc, etc.

A Camera
(or, even better, a mobile phone with a camera)

The camera is useful not only for recording crime scenes, but also for photographing the unexpected stuff that turns up during an investigation: documents or objects you find, suspects you spot sneaking around with bags marked *swag* over their shoulder, and so on. Of course, you could carry a phone and a camera separately, but why not go for the less-to-cart-about option?

Magnifying Glass

It might look a bit nerdy to go around blinking a huge eye through one of these, but a magnifying glass is a genuinely useful thing to have with you! Without it you could easily miss tell-tale scratches, loose fibres or other evidence.

Home-made Fingerprint Kit

(See page 227.)

Rubber Gloves

For wearing in situations where you might disturb fingerprints or other delicate evidence. Ordinary yellow washing-up-type gloves are fine, but those smaller see-through ones you can get in supermarkets are much cooler. Plus, when you're done, you can snap them off your hands and look *really* cool, like someone medical in a TV drama.

Evidence Bags

Real cops put everything into little plastic bags. You could use small-size paper bags, or maybe those thin transparent sandwich bags, or you could recycle various types of food packaging (as long as it's clean!).

Tape Measure

You'd be surprised how often the size of things, or their distance apart, can be a clue. Measure a footprint, for instance, and you can work out the suspect's shoe size.

Something to Put All This In

You could stuff all your kit into your pockets, but then you risk either forgetting something, or running out of room, or both. Keep everything in one handy container, ready for action at a moment's notice. What sort of container? An old lunchbox or (quite large) pencil case is good if you want to keep your detective gear disguised. Perhaps a laptop case if you want to look technical, or a biscuit tin if you want to look slightly silly.

Saxby Smart's Homestudy Course: Lesson 1

<u>What's Happened?</u>
A wallet has been stolen from a customer at the café in the local park. The next day, you're called in to investigate by the café owner. He ran out of the café as soon as the theft was discovered, but saw nobody running away.

<u>The Scene of the Crime</u>
2.25 pm. You're standing on the path outside the café. It's sunny today, as it has been all week. A lawn leads from the path down to the bank of the river. There's a road bridge which crosses the river about fifty metres upstream, and across the river there's a large field full of very tall, pale-coloured grass. Ducks quack along the

water. There aren't many people about. You examine the lawn for footprints but find none.

<u>Witness 'A'</u>
You talk to Witness 'A', a girl you know from school. She says she arrived outside the café as the owner was disappearing inside, muttering angrily about stolen money. These are her exact words, as recorded in your notebook:

I was just going for a walk. When I heard the café owner grumbling, I realised something must have happened. I looked around, but couldn't see anything suspicious. I was standing right here on this spot. Then I noticed someone in the field across the river. He was hurrying and looking over his shoulder. It was a boy about my age with dark hair and he was wearing a black jacket, jeans and scruffy trainers. I'm absolutely sure of that.

You sit on a nearby bench and do some thinking. Is Witness A reliable? Do you now have some definite clues about the identity of the thief? Or do you have reason to believe that Witness A is making it all up? What do you think?

If Witness A was standing right here, by the café, she could well have seen someone hurrying across that field over the river. But the field is full of very tall grass. How could she possibly know that anyone in that field was wearing scruffy trainers? They could have worn trainers, wellies, or glittery pink boots for all she knew.

<u>Conclusion</u>
Witness A is making it up.

ORGANISE
YOUR NOTEBOOK

Telling you to keep your detective notebook organised might sound obvious, but you'd be surprised how vitally important it can be to keep your thoughts down on paper in a logical, easy-to-find format. Here are a few useful pointers:

Notebook? What Notebook?

Flip-over jotter pad? Small ring binder? Beautifully bound and jaw-droppingly expensive designer thingummy with off-white paper? It's entirely up to you. The point is: be comfortable with your notebook. Whether you use an el cheapo scribble pad from the newsagent's or one of those fiddly posh ones with tie-up tassles and little bits carved out of the pages doesn't matter. What matters is that it suits *you*. And that it fits into your pocket or detective-type bag, of course!

Make It Personal

Following on from point 1, it's important to make sure that your notes are sorted the way *you* want them. There are many methods for note-organising: feel free to ignore them. As long as your notes make complete sense to you, anything goes.

1. You could use lots of abbreviations if you like (as long as you can remember what they mean!).

2. You could use underlining to signify only one specific thing (something that needs following up later, for example).

3. You could use symbols as a quick way to tag information (a '#' symbol to mark your No.1 suspect, for instance, or a '*' against a witness statement you've worked out is definitely true).

Cross-referencing

One very useful trick is to *number* the pages of your notebook. During most investigations, you'll find you need to refer back to previous info, or keep a particular listing to hand. Being able to put something like 'see page

12' against data in your notebook is much easier than having to put 'this bit links to that series of observations I wrote down last week sometime, maybe Tuesday'.

Colour-coding

Another hugely useful trick is to colour-code information where possible. Mark all crime scene notes in blue, for example, or the names of suspects in yellow. This sort of thing helps you to identify information quickly. You might end up with one clue marked in half a dozen colours or more, but that's OK: it probably shows how important that clue is!

For colour coding you could use:

- Highlighter pens
- Little stickers
- One of those pens with six or seven colours in it.

The Complete Picture

This is the most important thing of all: DON'T MISS ANYTHING (see Stage 6 of 'How to Investigate a Crime Scene' on page 215). Time and time again, an entire investigation can revolve around something which, at first, appeared to be a minor little detail. It's much better to keep a note of even the most trivial of things and then be able to cross it out later, than to have missed that detail in the first place.

Oh No! Teachers Are Right!

It's a terrible thing to have to admit, but the way teachers go on and on about neatness *is* actually important when it comes to being a brilliant schoolkid detective. What's the point of having detailed, cleverly argued notes if you can't actually *read* them? Yes, the clock is often ticking when you're on a case, but don't get flustered. Be cool, be logical . . . and, er, write neatly.

Online vs Paper

There are lots of online note-taking and note-organising services available on the internet. Are they a good idea?

On the plus side:

• Online notes are accessible from a lot of devices.

• Online notes save you having to carry notebook and pen around.

• Online notes can't be dropped or lost like written notes.

On the minus side:

• You still need to carry some sort of device around!

• What if your device runs out of power, or can't access the web from where you are? You're stuck!

• Online notes might be hacked by villains; you may find written notes are easier to look after.

Review. And Review Again.

Go through your notebook *regularly*. While you're on a case, you need to run through evidence every day *at the least*. It's when you review information that you'll most often spot connections you hadn't seen before, and get ideas that wouldn't otherwise have occurred to you. As you go through your notes, you can mark up data, compile a case file To Do list, and assess how far you've got in your investigations.

How to Investigate a Crime Scene (like the cops)

Someone is in need of your astonishing deductive powers! You race to the scene! But what should you do first? How can you be sure that you've examined every last piece of evidence?

What you'll need:
Your detective toolkit (see page 201)
Your astonishing deductive powers

Stage 1
Secure the scene. If you're investigating, for example, a theft from the school office, make sure nobody else

comes in or out of the office until your detective work is done. This is vitally important. You need to examine the scene as soon after the crime is discovered as possible. You don't want people walking around, disturbing evidence all over the place!

Stage 2

Photograph the scene. This means photographing everything – the overall scene, individual objects, footprints, anything that might be relevant. You never know when some small detail will become a crucial part of your investigation – better to take loads of pictures and not need them, than to only take a couple of pics and miss an important clue.

Stage 3

Sketch the scene. It's always useful to have a diagram showing the positions of things you've photographed. For instance, using our school office theft example, you might note the positions of muddy footmarks and see that the thief was running rather than walking. Or, you might notice that an object has been dropped too far from the desk to have been simply knocked over – was it scattered by the thief in a hurry? Could the thief have handled it and left fingerprints?

Stage 4

Gather prints or other evidence. Collect fingerprints as shown on page 227. Is there anything else the thief left behind? Does that sweet wrapper belong to someone in the office, or might the thief have dropped it? Is the office light on now, when it was left switched off? Does the arrangement of papers or objects suggest that the thief was searching the place? Has nothing else been disturbed, suggesting that the thief knew what they were looking for? Be alert! All sorts of things could give you a clue to what happened or who did it.

Stage 5

Take statements from witnesses. Maybe two pupils saw a figure running away from the office, or perhaps a teacher heard a noise when they thought the office was empty? Make sure you speak to each person involved SEPARATELY. Why? To make sure each person tells you what *they* saw or heard, and are not influenced by what others might say. The small differences between witness statements can reveal a lot! (After all, one of them might be lying. One of them might be the thief!) You must also interview anyone who might be able to provide useful information, whether they were a witness or not. For example, the school secretary might have been in the staff room and have seen nothing, but her knowledge of the office could tell you if something's been moved, or if something is missing that you hadn't taken account of.

Stage 6

Before you leave the scene, check over your notes. Are they clear? Are they as complete as possible? Remember, you can't come back later and start again!

Saxby Smart's Homestudy Course: Lesson 2

What's Happened?

A nearby bank has been robbed. The gang who did it have split up and gone into hiding. Meanwhile, a friend from school suspects that a man who's been renting the attic flat in the building where your friend lives is one of the thieves in disguise. You investigate.

The Suspect

9.44 am. You knock at the door of the attic flat, which is answered by The Suspect. He's a tall, well-dressed person, who speaks in a posh accent. You glance past him. The flat is one large room with a kitchen area at one end and a tiny, partitioned-off bathroom at the other. It's very neat, with a rug covering most of the floor and a broad window letting in a flood of daylight. Apart from a bed and a small wardrobe, there's just a TV and a few shelves of assorted books and movies. Several rather ugly abstract paintings hang on the bare white walls.

You pretend you're doing a survey for a school project. You enquire if you can ask The Suspect a few questions. The Suspect agrees, and the conversation is as follows:

<u>You</u>: What do you do for a living?

<u>Suspect (turning around and pointing to the paintings)</u>: I'm an artist. These are a small sample of my work.

<u>You</u>: You work from home?

<u>Suspect</u>: Yes. The view across the town from my window is always an inspiration.

<u>You</u>: Have you always wanted to be an artist?

<u>Suspect</u>: Yes, definitely. Ever since I first visited the Louvre museum in New York as a small child, I've loved the world of art. Painting is my whole life.

<u>You</u>: That's really interesting, thanks for your help, and your time.

<u>Suspect</u>: Not at all. Hope the school project goes well. Goodbye.

You scribble some notes and do some detective-style brainwork. Was your friend correct? Could The Suspect be hiding something? Or is he totally innocent, and exactly who he claims to be?

What do you think?

You have two distinct reasons to remain suspicious. First, The Suspect claims to be an artist, working from home, and yet there's not the slightest sign of it in that flat – no canvases, no paint, no artist's easel, not even a few splats of colour on the floor. Second, The Suspect got something completely wrong: the Louvre museum is in Paris, not New York (see the section about art theft on page 86) – no serious artist would make a mistake like that.

Conclusion

Your friend could be right. The Suspect needs further investigation.

How to Weigh Up Evidence

(or, Use Your Thinking Chair)

Whatever case you happen to be investigating, there will be three things that will always – always! – be present somewhere inside the tangle of clues, suspects and red herrings:

MOTIVE (in other words, *why* the crime happened): the culprit must have had a reason for committing the crime – it might be a strange, or flimsy, even crazy reason, but there'll be a reason for it somewhere.

METHOD (in other words, *how* the crime happened): this can be the trickiest part of a case – you need to work out the exact sequence of events which happened before, during and after the crime.

OPPORTUNITY (in other words, *when* the crime happened): timing requires careful attention – can you pinpoint the time of the crime and exactly where your suspects were at that time?

It's your job, as detective, to uncover the truth about these three things. And the best way to do that is simply to think: go through your notes, scrunch up your eyes in a really detectivey way, and use 'the little grey cells' as Hercule Poirot would say.

Your aim, as you sit in your Thinking Chair, is to work out where these three elements meet: to establish *who* amongst your list of suspects (or what sort of person, if you have no suspects yet!) *might* have had a reason to commit the crime, *and* a way of committing the crime, *and* the chance to commit the crime.

But Is This Enough?

Any police officer will tell you that working out motive, method and opportunity are not, by themselves, enough to prove a case. You'll also need **EVIDENCE**, to show that not only *could* your suspect have had the motive, method and opportunity, but that they also went ahead and actually *did* it!

Just because someone *might* have been involved, doesn't mean they *were*. Be both open-minded and logical at all times. Motive, method and opportunity point you in the right direction, but they can't solve the case alone!

Agatha Christie wrote a very good short story called 'Motive Vs Opportunity', which appears in her collection *The Thirteen Problems*. Have a look at that for more thoughts on this topic.

Saxby Smart's Homestudy Course: Lesson 3

<u>What's Happened?</u>
With the help of your evidence, the bank robbers from Lesson 2 have been rounded up. However, the location of the hiding place they've used for the stolen banknotes is still a mystery. Your investigations have narrowed it down to one of three possibilities.

<u>Possibility 1: A Canal Tunnel Beneath a Busy Road</u>
The tunnel is long and very dark, a perfect place to hide something because few people ever go through it. You have to scramble down the embankment at the side of the road to reach the entrance. Inside the tunnel, the dark water of the canal ripples gently. The sound of dripping

echoes off the low, semi-circular brick arch above, and the smell of damp hugs your nose. Green stuff grows between the bricks, some of which have come loose over the years. Here and there, a drainage grille gurgles softly as water moves through it. All you can clearly see in the tunnel is the light at each end.

Possibility 2: A Boarded-up House on the Edge of Town
The house is quite small and stands on its own beside a line of trees. All the windows and doors were boarded-up many years ago, and the whole place is surrounded by a knotted tangle of weeds where once there was a garden. There are ragged patches across the walls where paint has peeled away, leaving grooves for spiders and woodlice to nest in. The thick board covering the front door has become creased and flaking with age. The round, shiny silver heads of nails show around its edge, beside older, festering nail holes. A scattering of broken glass litters the ground and an empty drinks can tumbles around until it's trapped by the thorny undergrowth.

Possibility 3: A Burnt-out Van at the Local Rubbish Tip
It was once a large delivery van, but now it lies on its side, two wheels creaking slowly in the wind. The back doors are loose, it's not difficult to get inside. There are a couple of seats lolling in mid air, their backs ripped open.

A pile of old crates, empty and split, fill one corner. A lonely clipboard, with torn and cold-wrinkled paperwork still attached to it, dangles from a hook.

You retreat to your Crime HQ and rub your chin in a detectivey way. There's just one tiny clue which suggests that one of these possibilities might indeed be the bank robbers' hiding place.

Have you spotted it?

Take another look at the front door of that house. If the place was boarded up years ago, why are there shiny, silver nail heads showing? Are they new? Has someone removed that board and then put it back again, having to use new nails to fix it in place? Is that why there are older nail holes there too?

(The tunnel might seem a good hiding place at first, but it's so dark in there – could you ever be sure you'd find what you'd hidden? Besides, there's so much moisture in the tunnel that hiding banknotes might not be the best idea. The van would also seem a likely choice, but it's right by the local tip – there's far too much chance of accidental discovery there, or even of the van being dragged away and recycled!)

Conclusion

The most likely hiding place is the boarded-up house because there's evidence that someone's been there recently.

HOW TO FIND FINGERPRINTS
(USING EVERYDAY STUFF)

You're at the scene of a crime! Some low-life has hunted through the room in search of valuables! You're pretty sure he's left incriminating dabs all over the place, but how can you find them and keep them as evidence?

What you'll need:

A couple of pencils

A coin

A brush with very soft bristles

Sticky tape (transparent, not the brown stuff you use on parcels!)

Some card or pieces of paper

An adult with a small knife or potato peeler

Stage 1

Locate objects which may have prints on them. Hard, smooth surfaces are good for retaining finger marks – painted or varnished wood, most metals, shiny paper, that sort of thing. An empty glass is ideal, because most people wrap their fingers right around them. Soft, bumpy surfaces like soft furnishings or clothing rarely give good results. Handle the items carefully or you'll rub off the crook's prints and replace them with your own!

Stage 2

Now you need to grind down the graphite from your pencils. Using a knife or potato peeler, split or shave the wood to get at the graphite. Then crush the graphite as much as you can, using the coin on a flat surface. You're aiming to produce as fine a powder as possible.

TIP 1: If you don't want to use a knife, or ruin your pencils, get hold of some of those loose refills you can buy for propelling pencils.

TIP 2: If you live somewhere with an old-fashioned fireplace, soot would do just as well. But beware, it's messy!

Stage 3 (The Fiddly Bit)

Sprinkle the graphite powder on to the area where you think there's a fingerprint. As long as you've crushed the graphite down enough, you should see the powder start to stick to the print. The fine, dark powder stays attached to the semi-transparent oils left by your suspect's skin.

Stage 4 (The Even More Fiddly Bit!)

Take the soft brush – toothbrushes and nail brushes are hopeless, you need something delicate – and *very* gently brush at the area around the print. This will get rid of the excess graphite, leaving a clear fingerprint.

TIP: If you can't find a *really* soft brush, just blow softly around the print.

Stage 5 (The Fiddliest Bit of the Lot!)

Take a strip of sticky tape. Hold it at each end, sticky side facing away from you. Carefully place the tape over the fingerprint. Press it down veeeeery delicately. Then slowly peel it away. With a bit of luck, the powder-coated fingerprint will come off with it.

Stage 6

Now stick the tape down on to a piece of card or paper. The print should be visible as a powdery outline. You can use this preserved fingerprint as evidence to match against the inky-finger-on-paper prints of your suspect.

Saxby Smart's Homestudy Course: Lesson 4

What's Happened?

The school's worst bully and his friends have planned to ambush a group of your classmates outside school. You haven't been able to find out where or when. Then you discover a strange, handwritten note.

You have the note flat out on the kitchen table in front of you. However much you stare at it, it still looks like total gibberish:

UPNPSSPX SJHIU BGUFS TDIPPM PVUTJEF HBUFT

As far as you can see, one of three methods for decoding the message should be the right one . . .

Method 1 – Substitution

You always use one particular letter to replace another. For example, R is always replaced with Y, B is always replaced with Q and so on. Very difficult to crack, if you don't know what's being substituted for what!

Method 2 – Letter Skipping

Only certain letters are part of the message, the rest is just padding. You take every other letter, or every fourth letter, etc. Easier to crack!

Method 3 – Letter Shifting

Every letter in the message is shifted a specific number of letters up or down the alphabet. If you shift everything back by three letters, for example, E would always be B, W would always be T, etc. Not hard to crack, once you've worked out the number of letters being shifted.

You scratch your head for a few moments, then find a pen. This is going to need some careful, logical, detective-type reasoning. Can you work it out?

The method which works is number 3. All the letters in the message have been shifted one letter forwards in the alphabet – you just read one letter back each time to reveal the correct words.

Conclusion

The message reads, **TOMORROW RIGHT AFTER SCHOOL OUTSIDE GATES.**

RED ALERT!
KNOWN CON-TRICKS
TO WATCH OUT FOR

The famous American circus showman P. T. Barnum once said, 'There's a sucker born every minute', meaning there's no shortage of gullible people you can trick money out of. (Actually, Barnum didn't say that, it was a journalist called David Hannum, but it's the sort of thing Barnum would have said.)

All brilliant schoolboy detectives need to be aware of a whole range of confidence tricks that have been fooling people for years. Why? Because knowing about such things is often a good short-cut to solving a mystery, when the villain you're up against is equally knowledgeable on con-trickery!

Here are some prominent sneaky schemes to watch out for:

Pig-In-A-Poke

Perhaps the oldest recorded con-trick, dating from medieval times. The person doing the conning (the 'con') shows a small pig in a bag to the one who's being conned (the 'mark'). The mark pays for a pig of their own and they're given a bag with a wriggling animal inside. The animal turns out to be a cat, not a pig. This con is the origin of the phrases 'buying a pig in a poke' and 'letting the cat out of the bag'.

Get Rich Quick Schemes

There are *loads* of these: basically, anything which offers you the chance to get lots of money for very little effort is one of these cons. How to Get Rich courses, chain letters, fortune tellers selling lucky charms, they're all variations on this idea. A good example is an American called Victor Lustig, who sold people money-printing machines. He'd demonstrate to the mark how the machine produced a $100 note. Yippee, says the mark, I'm rich, and hands over a bucketload of cash. The machine produces another couple of $100, giving Lustig time to get away . . . and then churns out nothing but blank paper. The really sneaky bit: since the mark was willing to do something illegal (print their own money!) they couldn't go to the cops without admitting they'd tried to break the law.

Salting the Mine

In this type of con, the mark is tricked into thinking that a worthless hole in the ground is a gold mine. The cons place a small amount of gold in the hole (perhaps using a shotgun to blast it into the ground), then allow the mark to accidentally-on-purpose discover the gold traces. The mark thinks he's going to make a fortune, and buys the land from the cons for a vastly inflated price. The cons pretend they've no knowledge of the gold and make their exit leaving the mark thinking HE'S the one who's conned THEM!

The Nigerian Bank Scam

This one is *very* common on the internet. The mark receives an email claiming to be from an overseas bank. Oh deary me, says the 'bank', we need to temporarily shift several million bucks to a foreign person to avoid a dreadful crash that will ruin our beloved country, please, please help us! All you've got to do is send us details of your bank account and we'll transfer the money. You can keep a million as a reward. Spot the flaw? The mark sends their bank info and the cons simply empty their account.

Phishing

Also *very* common on the web – this is one which catches a lot of people out. Beware! The mark receives an email which *seems* to be from an organisation they've heard of and possibly deal with regularly – an online shop, for example, a bank or an auction site. The email says: Oh woe, oh horror, your account with us is in big trouble! Internet crooks have hacked in! (Of course, the ones sending the email are the crooks, and they've made the email look just like one you might get from the real bank shop, etc.) Send us your account info, they say, to 'confirm who you are' or to 're-activate' your account. The mark sends back an email, or clicks on a link and fills in a form on a fake site, and now the cons have got enough information to commit identity theft. (The basic rule here is: never, ever, ever, send personal information anywhere, ever, without being SURE who it's going to.)

Gold Brick Scams

In this con, the mark is sold something for far more money than it's worth. For example, a guy in a van is selling stuff at the local market. My boss got delivered too many of these TVs by mistake, he says. I've got a load of them here I can sell really cheap, they're fine, it's just that the factory sent us more than we ordered without charging us. Good, eh? How many d'ya want?

Hmm, thinks the mark, what a bargain! He buys one of the con's huge cardboard boxes . . . only to find, when he gets it home, it's a broken old load of rubbish.

Another version of this is the 'Thai Gems' scam: tourists in a foreign country are persuaded to buy jewellery (or something similar), being told it's much cheaper here than at home because of overseas taxes. The tourists get home to discover the jewellery is next to worthless (or agree to have the stuff mailed to them 'to avoid import duties' and find it never arrives)!

The Melon Drop

So called because cons in Europe discovered that melons were very expensive in Japan and played this trick on Japanese tourists, using melons. The con deliberately bumps into the mark and drops a box (containing something already broken) which then 'smashes' against the pavement. Oh no, cries the con, that was my dead auntie's valuable favourite heirloom! How could you! The mark, feeling terribly guilty, pays up for a replacement.

The Bug-in-My-Soup Trick

The con, dressed in expensive clothes, goes into a posh restaurant. Halfway through the meal, the con takes a live bug from their pocket and drops it on to their vegetables. 'Ahhghhh! What's this?' screams the con. 'I thought this place was a high-quality restaurant! Look everyone, vermin in my food! Ahhhghhhh!' The manager of the restaurant, to shut the con up and avoid a scandal, gives the con his meal for free.

The Football Picks Scam

This is a complicated one – pay attention! The con sends out a prediction for an upcoming game to a hundred sports fans. Half the predictions say Team A will win, half say Team B. After the game, the con then knows who he's sent the correct predictions to. He sends *them* another prediction for an upcoming game, again predicting a win for one team or the other. Once *that* game has been played, the con does the whole thing again, sending predictions to the ones he now knows he's correctly predicted *two* games for. After another couple of rounds of so-called predictions, the con is left with a handful of fans for whom he has apparently correctly 'predicted' four wins in a row. He says, this is all down to my new sure-fire sports-prediction system. You can't lose! A win every time! The fans who've received all these correct predictions think, hmmm, maybe he's right, after all he's sent me *four* correct predictions. (Of course, these few fans don't know about all the other, many fans who have, by chance, NOT received those predictions.) At this point, the con strikes: I've got *another* sure-fire prediction, he says. You could make a fortune using my prediction to bet money on! But I've proved my system works, so this time you have to pay for it. Please send me a bucketful of cash. Out of that small group of fans, one or two may fall for it and send the money. At which point, the con-man makes his exit.

The Pigeon Drop Technique

Again, there are a number of versions of this one. The most common scam goes like this: Con A goes into a shop. Help me, Shop Assistant, I've lost my ring! I must have dropped it, it's worth a fortune. Everyone looks around. Of course, no ring has been dropped anywhere. Con A says, I've got to go, here's my mobile number, please keep looking Shop Assistant, if you find it I'll give you a reward of £1000. I'll come back later. Con A leaves, and a couple of minutes later Con B enters the shop. Hey, look, someone's dropped a ring here, says Con B. Ooooh, says Shop Assistant, thank you, I know who owns that, I'll give it back to them. Hang on, says Con B, I found it. This looks very valuable, I bet the owner would give me a reward, I'm keeping it for now. Shop Assistant thinks he's going to miss the reward! Tell you want, he says, I'll give you £500 for the ring. That way, YOU get a reward, and I get to return it. Hmmm, OK says Con B, fair enough, and hands over the ring. Ho ho, thinks Shop Assistant, I'm still £500 up on the deal! He rings the mobile number . . . to find it doesn't exist. He takes the ring to a jeweller . . . to find it's worth about a fiver. Meanwhile, Con A and Con B have run off with the £500.

The Car Park Trick

The con finds an empty patch of land in the middle of a city, puts on a uniform and starts charging motorists to park there for the day. As soon as any genuine official appears, the con makes his exit, leaving all the cars parked illegally.

There are many, MANY con-tricks out there. The above is just the tiniest little selection of the hundreds of ways in which cons are willing to make marks of us all. Keep a sharp eye out!

A LOOK ALONG SAXBY'S SHELVES

Here are some suggestions for further reading (apart from the Saxby Smart case files, of course . . .) and a selection of great cops 'n' robbers films and TV series.

You should be able to find most, if not all, of these in online or high street book and DVD retailers, or through your local public library.

Saxby

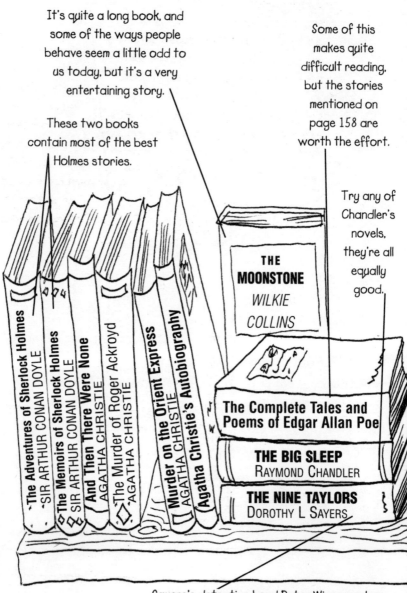

It's quite a long book, and some of the ways people behave seem a little odd to us today, but it's a very entertaining story.

These two books contain most of the best Holmes stories.

Some of this makes quite difficult reading, but the stories mentioned on page 158 are worth the effort.

Try any of Chandler's novels, they're all equally good.

THE MOONSTONE
WILKIE COLLINS

The Complete Tales and Poems of Edgar Allan Poe

THE BIG SLEEP RAYMOND CHANDLER

THE NINE TAYLORS DOROTHY L SAYERS

The Adventures of Sherlock Holmes — SIR ARTHUR CONAN DOYLE

The Memoirs of Sherlock Holmes — SIR ARTHUR CONAN DOYLE

And Then There Were None — AGATHA CHRISTIE

The Murder of Roger Ackroyd — AGATHA CHRISTIE

Murder on the Orient Express — AGATHA CHRISTIE

Agatha Christie's Autobiography

Sayers's detective Lord Peter Wimsey solves the 20-year mystery of some missing gems.

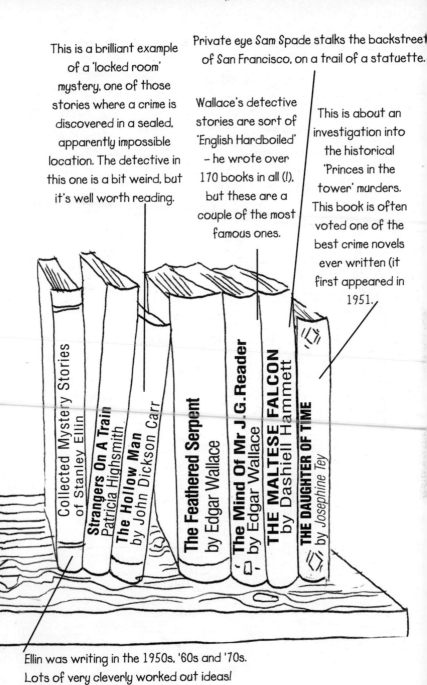

This is a brilliant example of a 'locked room' mystery, one of those stories where a crime is discovered in a sealed, apparently impossible location. The detective in this one is a bit weird, but it's well worth reading.

Private eye Sam Spade stalks the backstreets of San Francisco, on a trail of a statuette.

Wallace's detective stories are sort of 'English Hardboiled' – he wrote over 170 books in all (!), but these are a couple of the most famous ones.

This is about an investigation into the historical 'Princes in the tower' murders. This book is often voted one of the best crime novels ever written (it first appeared in 1951.

Collected Mystery Stories of Stanley Ellin

Strangers On A Train Patricia Highsmith

The Hollow Man by John Dickson Carr

The Feathered Serpent by Edgar Wallace

The Mind Of Mr J.G.Reader by Edgar Wallace

THE MALTESE FALCON by Dashiell Hammett

THE DAUGHTER OF TIME by Josephine Tey

Ellin was writing in the 1950s, '60s and '70s.
Lots of very cleverly worked out ideas!

A LOOK ALONG SAXBY'S SHELVES: MOVIES AND TV SERIES

The 1974 version is a very good dramatisation of the book.

This is about con men in America during the Great Depression. Listen out for some great Hardboiled slang! (But whatever you do, don't go near The Sting II – it's rubbish.)

This one is (loosely!) based on the true story of Frank Abagnale, who tricked his way into all kinds of things in the 1960s.

A mild-mannered bank clerk joins in with a scheme to steal gold bullion.

Not exactly an accurate representation of the era of Public Enemies! But it does give you a flavour of the 1920s and 1930s in America.

A retired crook gathers his gang together for one last robbery! A great film full of Hardboiled atmosphere!

THE LAVENDER HILL MOB (1951)

MURDER ON THE ORIENT EXPRESS (1974)

THE STING (1973)

CATCH ME IF YOU CAN (2002)

BUGSY MALONE (1976)

THE ASPHALT JUNGLE (1950)

Not what you might think from the title! The plot is put together in a very clever bits-and-pieces way. The story is about a robbery at a horseracing track.

The original version starring Michael Caine, NOT the remake! This film features a very clever gold bullion robbery, A brilliant car chase, and a real cliffhanger ending . . .

If you feel like watching something really silly . . . Both these movies feature a totally useless French detective called Inspector Clouseau. There are others movies featuring Clouseau too, but these are the funniest.

This series, starring David Suchet, includes adaptations of almost all Christie's Hercule Poirot stories.

The one made in the 1980s starring Jeremy Brett is most people's favourite.

THE KILLING (1956)

THE ITALIAN JOB (1969)

A SHOT IN THE DARK (1964)

RETURN OF THE PINK PANTHER (1975)

AGAHA CHRISTIE'S POIROT

SHERLOCK HOLMES

COLOMBO

Colombo is a brilliant example of the back-to-front plot: in every episode you see who did it straight away, then watch as the detective untangles the truth!

SAXBY SMART
PRIVATE DETECTIVE

Be the sleuth yourself and crack all the cases!

In each story Saxby Smart – schoolboy detective – gives you, the reader, clues which help solve the mystery. Are you 'smart' enough to find the answers?

Praise for the *Saxby Smart* series:

'Talk about feeling involved in a book! . . . Shortish, sharp reads written in a lively and snappy style.' *Liverpool Echo*

'. . . wise-cracking, engaging style, reminiscent of the Sherlock Holmes stories.' *School Librarian*

'This is a fun read made even more enjoyable by being able to turn detective yourself.' *Primary Times*

'The case files are challenging and all three stories are gently amusing and genuinely puzzling.' *Carousel*,

'It is hard not to be engaged . . . because the reader has to help this schoolboy detective piece together the clues.' *Daily Mail*

The **Curse** of the **Ancient** Mask

A mysterious curse, suspicious sabotage of a school competition, and a very unpleasant relative all conspire to puzzle Saxby Smart, schoolboy private detective.

Case files include: *The Curse of the Ancient Mask, The Mark of the Purple Homework* and *The Clasp of Doom*.

The **Fangs** of the **Dragon**

A string of break-ins where nothing is stolen, a rare comic book snatched from an undamaged safe, and clues apparently leading to a hidden treasure – Saxby solves three more challenging crimes.

Case files include: *The Fangs of the Dragon, The Tomb of Death* and *The Treasure of Dead Man's Lane*.

The Pirate's Blood

A bloody handprint inside a museum case containing pirate treasure, a classmate with a mysterious secret, and a strange case of arson in a bookshop require Saxby's help.

Case files include: *The Pirate's Blood*, *The Mystery of Mary Rogers* and *The Lunchbox of Notre Dame*.

The Hangman's Lair

A terrifying visit to the Hangman's Lair , a serious threat of blackmail, and a mystery surrounding a stranger's unearthly powers test Saxby to the limit !

Case files include: *The Hangman's Lair*, *Diary of Fear* and *Whispers from the Dead*.

The Eye of the Serpent

A valuable work of art vanishes into thin air, a notorious crook returns from the dead, and there's an eerie case of stolen identity . . . Time to call in Saxby Smart!

Case files include: *The Eye of the Serpent*, *The Ghost at the Window* and *The Stranger in the Mirror*.

Five Seconds to Doomsday

Saxby's arch-enemy plots his ultimate revenge, video games vanish off a truck, and the school office is the target of an apparently pointless robbery. What's really going on?

Case files include: *Five Seconds to Doomsday*, *March of the Zombies* and *The Shattered Box*.

The Poisoned Arrow

Everything's backwards! Saxby must stop a sinister crime *before* it happens, prove the innocence of a suspect who says they are guilty, and outcheat a team on a school quiz!

Stories include: *The Poisoned Arrow*, *The Nightmare of Room 9B* and *The Final Problem*.

Secret of the Skull

Saxby's most thrilling case files to date – with a sinister aunty, diamond smugglers and one very angry teacher!

Stories include: *Secret of the Skull*, *Diamonds Are For Heather* and *The Guy Who Came In From The Cold*.

saxbysmart.co.uk

Featuring an exclusive
online mystery to solve!

Plus:
Saxby Newsletter
Competitions
Ask the Author
Book Disguisers
Writing Tips
and much more!